Heartland Blues

Heartland Blues

Labor Rights in the Industrial Midwest

MARC DIXON

OXFORD
UNIVERSITY PRESS

Oxford University Press is a department of the University of Oxford. It furthers
the University's objective of excellence in research, scholarship, and education
by publishing worldwide. Oxford is a registered trade mark of Oxford University
Press in the UK and certain other countries.

Published in the United States of America by Oxford University Press
198 Madison Avenue, New York, NY 10016, United States of America.

Library of Congress Cataloging-in-Publication Data
Names: Dixon, Marc, 1974– author.
Title: Heartland blues : labor rights in the industrial Midwest /
Marc Dixon, Department of Sociology, Dartmouth College.
Description: New York, NY : Oxford University Press, [2020] |
Includes bibliographical references and index.
Identifiers: LCCN 2020020749 (print) | LCCN 2020020750 (ebook) |
ISBN 9780190917036 (hardback) | ISBN 9780190917067 (oso) |
ISBN 9780190917050 (epub) | ISBN 9780190917043 (updf)
Subjects: LCSH: Labor movement—Middle West—History—20th century. |
Collective bargaining—Middle West—History—20th century. | Collective
labor agreements—Middle West—History—20th century. |
Labor unions—Middle West—History—20th century.
Classification: LCC HD8083.M53.D59 2020 (print) |
LCC HD8083.M53 (ebook) | DDC 331.880977/09045—dc23
LC record available at https://lccn.loc.gov/2020020749
LC ebook record available at https://lccn.loc.gov/2020020750

1 3 5 7 9 8 6 4 2

Printed by Sheridan Books, Inc., United States of America

Contents

Figures and Tables

Figures

Tables

unions are important

bad news brums   PATCO

Preface

This book grew out of conversations with colleagues and friends in 2011 and 2012. Many asked me about what was going on in Wisconsin and other Midwestern states where union rights were rolled back. Protests had erupted across the region. Unions were front-page news again, though most of it was bad news for the labor movement. Unions were losing in what were once union strongholds. It all sounded vaguely familiar. It was not necessarily a repeat of labor's historical lowlights, like President Reagan's firing of the air traffic controllers in 1981 or the organizing failures and freefall in union membership that began in the 1970s. Scholars have identified both as critical turning points in recent labor history. Rather, labor's unraveling in the Midwest reminded me of what many would consider a happier time in labor relations—the 1950s. I had written about the adoption of anti-labor laws across states following the New Deal, including the encroachment of these laws into the industrial Midwest in the 1950s when unions were strongest.[1] Then too ambitious politicians and new conservative organizations chock-full of money sought to curb union rights and sparked significant labor opposition. But I had moved on to other projects by the time anti-union activities heated up in this very same place in the 2010s. As I began to dig around a bit, it was clear there was lot of action on labor politics that I and other scholars had missed or underestimated. It was worth revisiting, and so I did.

Full disclosure: this book is motivated not only by research questions central to social scientists, which I take up in the following chapters, but by my belief that unions are important. For all their warts, unions were one of the most significant equalizing forces of the last century. Scholars are just now grappling with the far-reaching consequences of their decline in the United States. Sophisticated statistical analyses that account for a host of potentially confounding factors show how union decline has contributed to several pressing social problems, including growing income inequality and increases in poverty among households with employed individuals, or what social scientists call "working poverty." Union decline has weakened the middle class and diminished an important pathway of upward social mobility from

anti-New Deal

Social movement

one generation to the next. It has contributed, at least indirectly, to the out-sized influence of elite and corporate interests on government.[2]

More generally, unions provide average workers with a voice; they offer some protection against the whims of an abusive boss and the swings of the labor market. In their classic 1984 book *What Do Unions Do?*, economists Richard Freeman and James Medoff described unions as having two faces. One is the monopoly face, which can produce inefficiencies and breed cor-ruption. The other is the voice face, which gives workers some say over their livelihood and collective representation at work and in politics. They find the positive voice effects to generally outweigh the negative monopoly effects. Without unions, employees have less say about what they do at work every day and less control over their lives. Not all unions live up to these lofty standards, of course, but it is my belief that a robust and democratic labor movement gives workers a better shot.[3]

For all these reasons, I think the decline of labor unions is a bad thing. Those who do not share this view should still be interested in some of the consequences of union decline. The absence of labor or an equally forceful social movement to advocate for the least well-off or for those left behind by economic globalization and technological advancements opens the door to all sorts of demagoguery. It is therefore important to understand why unions are in decline and that the roots of this decline lie not only in the economic crises of the 1970s, as much scholarship suggests, but that it goes back fur-ther. Even when unions were big and times seemingly were good, unions still struggled to translate power in numbers into political influence or so-cial acceptance. Perhaps because it is so hard to imagine a powerful labor movement today, we tend to misremember the historical peak of union mem-bership in the 1950s in broad-brush terms, as a golden age or when America was great. Leaning too heavily on nostalgia is never good because we tend to get the story wrong. The heyday of American unionism was marked by considerable conflict. Business and labor fought over union rights, and not all of these conflicts went labor's way. Understanding the conditions under which unions succeeded or failed during this period of exceptional strength reveals many obstacles to union influence that became more apparent in the following decades. This book provides such an understanding by revisiting political conflicts over labor rights in America's industrial heartland in the 1950s. It is my hope that this not only helps get the 1950s story right, but that it provides a critical historical perspective for understanding unions today and their tough road ahead.

goes back further

I am writing this book for scholars of labor and social movements and those in closely related fields, for people who care about unions, and for individuals who haven't thought much about unions before but may care deeply about inequality, democracy, or dignity at work. Because I trace the factors shaping who wins and loses in conflicts over labor rights, this book contributes to the study of contentious politics more generally, whether or not one is motivated by the fate of unions today or the consequences of their decline. Some chapters may be more helpful than others depending on one's perspective. Whereas the meat of the book (chapters 2–5) follows labor in the 1950s, chapters 6 and 7 bring the focus closer to the present by considering how the focal labor policies fared in subsequent decades and how the weaknesses unions exhibited in the 1950s continue to pose problems today. I highlight these different contributions and options for reading in the next chapter. In the aim of clarity and accessibility, I relegate most technical language, genealogy of subfield-type material, and other specialized debates to endnotes and to other work.

In writing this book, I have benefitted from numerous conversations with colleagues and friends. I thank Elizabeth Choi, Sera Kwon, and Kate Wood for research assistance. I am grateful to Steve Boutcher, Bill Danaher, Jason Houle, Larry Isaac, Janice McCabe, Vinnie Roscigno, Tom Shriver, Suzanne Staggenborg, Alan Taylor, Dan Tope, and Anita Warren for their feedback. Matt Garcia, Christianne Hardy, Andrew Martin, Andrew Samwick, and Judith Stepan-Norris all provided helpful comments on the manuscript. John Campbell was an incredibly helpful sounding board throughout the process. I also benefitted from feedback on portions of the project in presentations at Dartmouth College, the Five Colleges Social Movements Working Group at Smith College, the University of Massachusetts, and the University of New Hampshire. Finally, the anonymous reviewers from Oxford University Press also provided invaluable suggestions, as did James Cook, my editor. Financial support for this book has come from the National Science Foundation and Dartmouth College's Nelson A. Rockefeller Center for Public Policy and the Department of Sociology.

Most of all, I am grateful to my wife and best friend, Melissa Horwitz, who read drafts, listened to any number of half-baked arguments and helped me make them better, and without whose support this work would not be possible.

1

Back to the Future

[handwritten: "If this wasn't the South after all"]

The one-time center of union strength was turned upside down at the beginning of 2011. In February of that year, Wisconsin governor Scott Walker introduced a budget bill that eliminated collective bargaining rights for public-sector workers and nearly sparked a revolt. First led by the Teaching Assistants' Association from the University of Wisconsin, protesters occupied the capitol. Democratic legislators then fled from Wisconsin to Illinois to deny Republicans a quorum. Not long after, Indiana Democrats fled to Illinois to prevent Republicans from passing right-to-work legislation there. By March, more than 100,000 protesters packed Capitol Square in Madison while tens of thousands of labor supporters marched on statehouses across the region. The sleepy Midwest was alive with protest.

With the conservative sweep of the 2010 midterm elections, a broad swath of the region's statehouses went Republican and many of them immediately set out to limit labor rights. Some bills were designed to eliminate public-sector collective bargaining rights entirely, as in Wisconsin and Ohio, or for particular groups, such as teachers, as in Indiana. Other bills, such as right-to-work laws, explicitly targeted union finances. Such laws posed a resource crunch for unions by prohibiting unions from compelling all workers to join or pay a representation fee despite a requirement to negotiate on their behalf. State legislatures also sought to repeal prevailing wage laws that set wage floors on publicly financed construction projects, undercutting the building trades unions. Other, more obscure bills made it difficult for liberal municipalities to pass minimum wage increases or other protective measures. All of this was met with considerable opposition, partly because the bills themselves were not popular, but also because of the place in which these changes occurred—the Midwest, the former industrial heartland. Here, unions and labor rights seemed at least minimally accepted. This wasn't the South, after all.[1]

What briefly looked like a labor uprising, however, soon turned into a rout. In Wisconsin, Republicans stripped the budget bill of its fiscal elements so it could proceed without a quorum and passed the new bill (Act 10) in the

Heartland Blues. Marc Dixon, Oxford University Press (2020). © Oxford University Press.
DOI: 10.1093/oso/9780190917036.001.0001.

middle of the night without the opposition present.[2] Labor and protesters launched a campaign to recall the governor, but this quickly lost steam. The opposition candidate had already lost to Walker once. President Obama's tepid support—a single tweet issued on Election Day—did not sway many Democrats. The effort failed at the polls and did not gain unions any goodwill in the process. Over the next few years, Republicans gained seats in the legislature and, burnishing his credentials for a presidential run, Scott Walker helped usher in a right-to-work law in early 2015.[3]

A mostly similar scene played out across the region. Ohio, a lone bright spot for unions in this drama, passed a bill similar to Wisconsin's Act 10 but then repealed it at the ballot box after labor and its allies launched a referendum campaign. In Indiana, the flight of Democratic legislators in 2011 temporarily tabled right-to-work, but it was not enough to stop restrictions on collective bargaining for public school teachers. After regrouping over the summer, the conservative coalition, now with governor Mitch Daniels's blessing, passed right-to-work legislation in early 2012, in time for Indianapolis to host its first Super Bowl. Michigan, the birthplace of the United Auto Workers, followed suit and passed their own right-to-work law in a lame duck legislative session at the end of the year.

For unions, things only got worse from there. The 2016 presidential election again brought focus to the Midwest. This time a large share of working-class voters turned away from unions and the Democratic Party to support Republican Donald Trump, helping to flip the pivotal states of Pennsylvania, Ohio, Michigan, and Wisconsin in his favor. In June 2018, the Supreme Court, with Trump appointee Neil Gorsuch, outlawed union security agreements in public-sector employment, effectively making a national right-to-work law for public employees. Similar cases, supported by a network of conservative donors and organizations, had been making their way through the court system for years. Illinois Republican governor Bruce Rauner sued to challenge public-sector union representation fees in 2015, but he was found to not have standing. The conservative State Policy Network found a more compelling plaintiff in Illinois state employee Mark Janus. He similarly contested his union's representation fee as a violation of his First Amendment rights. In a 5–4 decision, the high court sided with Janus that any public-sector union activity, including routine collective bargaining, constitutes political speech and cannot be coerced.[4]

How did the Midwest, once the center of union strength, become a hotbed for anti-unionism? Many early observations centered on union weakness and conservative ascendance in a post–Citizens United era of politics.[5] The ad hoc reflections in the wake of the protests mesh well with the extensive literature on union decline. Scholars have identified major political, economic, and cultural forces at work in the 1970s and 1980s that undermined the ability of unions to organize new members and bargain with employers. Globalization and technological change, financialization, the withering power of the strike, and mounting employer and conservative political opposition, not to mention unions' own missteps and organizing failures, are identified as key culprits for labor's long decline and its current weakness. While there is some debate on the impact of individual factors, the following is clear: Union decline accelerated in the 1970s, after which wages for average Americans flatlined and economic inequality began to expand. Employers became more militant in resisting union efforts during these years. Employer-led union decertification campaigns and strikebreaking increased in the 1970s and 1980s. The number of union-organizing attempts, which had held steady through the 1970s, fell off a cliff following President Reagan's firing of the air traffic controllers in 1981. Striking soon became a measure of last resort.[6]

Despite multiple leadership shakeups, the formation of new labor federation Change to Win in 2005, and considerable experimentation in organizing and outreach, unions have been unable to reverse these trends. By any metric—for example, membership density, organizing activity, strike frequency—the labor movement today is a shell of its mid-twentieth-century self. The percentage of the workforce belonging to unions has been nearly cut in half since the early 1980s. Private-sector unionization is below 7 percent. The title of Jake Rosenfeld's excellent book on the topic, *What Unions No Longer Do*, says it all. Through the lens of much labor scholarship, the fallout in the Midwest was long in the making, the result of a half century of union decline.[7]

The rich literature on union decline tells us many things about labor's plight and the tough road ahead, but it does not adequately explain the more recent labor failings in the Midwest. And it tends to obscure important vulnerabilities that unions have long exhibited. This is partly because many of these issues—right-to-work, public-sector bargaining, and fierce debates over the legitimacy of unions—predate labor's troubles in the 1970s and 1980s. Indeed, if I were to describe a scenario in which deep-pocketed conservatives resorted to unusual means to limit labor rights in a place where unions seemed accepted, this could as easily capture the industrial Midwest of the late 1950s as that of the 2010s. During the 1950s, Indiana, Ohio, and Wisconsin, all highly unionized states, were similarly at the forefront of debates over labor rights—this during a time described as the golden age of industrial capitalism and in a place marked by unparalleled union strength. Labor's recent troubles in the Midwest are more than a story about union weakness and decline. Consistent across these two very different periods is that union legitimacy was hotly contested.

This book takes a different track than the literature on union decline. I revisit labor at the peak of its strength in the 1950s. I examine campaigns over right-to-work laws and public-sector collective bargaining rights in Indiana, Ohio, and Wisconsin in the late 1950s—at the geographic center of union strength. I observe how unions and their opponents forged coalitions and developed support for policy proposals in the three focal states and across the region, and how they sought to convey a larger public stake in labor rights. I also gauge why union influence often was fleeting despite considerable resources. In many ways, the fights over labor rights in the 1950s were a dress rehearsal for the conservative onslaught in the decades to come. Business organizations honed right-to-work arguments as pro-worker. The modern regulatory framework for public-sector collective bargaining began to take shape during these years, but so too did the legal theories that ultimately would undermine it. The Midwest was front and center for all of this.

The focus on conflicts over labor rights in the 1950s is at odds with popular images of that decade. The 1950s captures the imagination of academics as a period when unions were strong, inequality was low, and it was a good time to be working class—at least if you were white and male. The power of nostalgia is strong. This hazy historical imagery of a prosperous and cohesive society has gained a much larger following with the political slogan Make America Great Again. For many, this was when America was truly great. As with any sweeping historical comparison, this conceals as much as it reveals. The real picture is, of course, more complicated.[8]

Revisiting Labor in the 1950s

Social science research on labor in the mid-twentieth century tends to veer in one of two directions. One strand of research stresses the importance of strong unions and stable collective bargaining between unions and large firms. The two to three decades after World War II have been retroactively described as a capital–labor accord, where unions were mostly accepted as "legitimate pillars of American working life."[9] Striking led to consistent wage gains for workers in manufacturing, construction, and other sectors where unions were strong. Unionized work in heavy industry did not eliminate poor working conditions or upend the race and gender hierarchies that privileged white male workers, but union gains were nonetheless widespread. Union-negotiated wage increases spilled over to nonunion workers and set the pace for many industries. The median worker saw their annual income double in the two decades following World War II. In the long history of the labor movement in the United States, this period was exceptional in many respects.[10]

Some of this was due to the hegemonic position of the United States after World War II. The United States emerged from the war with no real economic competitors. The Marshall Plan, which helped rebuild the war-torn economies of Europe, also provided new markets for American companies. There was a lot of surplus to go around. But this rising tide also had a social foundation in a unionized, Democratic voting bloc of blue-collar workers in mass production industries. Unlike prior gains unions achieved during World War I or the labor upsurges of the nineteenth century, this loose political coalition helped to preserve many of the gains labor achieved in the New Deal. The labor movement pushed the northern Democratic Party to be more pro-worker by supporting favorable candidates and policies at all levels of government, and to good effect. Labor became an important anchor of the Democratic Party. They were a countervailing power to corporate influence. For all these reasons, the decade serves as a key empirical benchmark for understanding just how far unions have fallen.[11]

Another body of research offers a more critical view of the period. Barry Eidlin's work on labor in the United States and Canada shows how New Deal policy that helped birth the industrial union movement also shaped a comparatively narrow and fragmented labor coalition. Other research shows how the Wagner Act institutionalized and in many ways muted labor militancy. It also excluded large groups of workers, particularly minorities. What is more, its implementation through the National Labor Relations Board (NLRB) stoked intra-class conflict between rival American Federation of Labor (AFL) and Congress of Industrial Organizations (CIO) labor federations. Political elites exacerbated these working-class fissures, while unions themselves abandoned broader progressive goals, such as national health insurance, in favor of private economic gains through collective bargaining.[12]

The incorporation of the labor movement into the New Deal state thus came with significant costs for unions. As unions became a part of mainstream life, they discarded some of their most forceful activists. Judith Stepan-Norris and Maurice Zeitlin's seminal works on labor and radicalism during the 1940s demonstrate how the purging of communists from industrial unions robbed the labor movement of its most energetic grassroots organizers, tenacious negotiators, and forceful backers of racial and gender equality. By the dawn of the 1950s, much of the "movement" seemed to be missing from the "labor movement." Instead, labor's actions were characterized by "business unionism," where unions functioned mostly as an insurance policy for workers, rather than as a forceful social movement. The first president of the merged AFL-CIO, the conservative George Meany of the plumbers union, who had never led a strike, is often singled out as the face of this narrow vision of unionism. From this more critical perspective, the period was marked as much by its missed opportunities as the impressive economic gains.[13]

Labor's move to the right occurred in a Cold War environment where the federal government and large corporations sought to expand American-style capitalism abroad and sometimes needed labor's help. Meany thus saw value in aligning his federation with the interests of large corporations and the federal government. As some European countries established codetermination structures after World War II, the AFL-CIO, with the help of the federal government, instead pushed for a narrower version of unionism in Latin America and elsewhere.[14] From its beginnings, the AFL-CIO stood out as the most conservative central labor body among advanced capitalist democracies. Its politically inspired commitment to free trade, which hardened in the early postwar years, persisted even as many large US firms moved to shed collective bargaining contracts in the face of increased international competition in the 1970s.[15]

Both literatures, while instructive, tend to underestimate the considerable resistance to unionism by the business community that persisted throughout the 1950s despite the conservative drift of the labor movement. For example, labor historians demonstrate how increased collective bargaining and rising prosperity did not preclude intense fights over unionism. Elizabeth Fones-Wolf details far-reaching community campaigns that the National Association of Manufacturers (NAM) and other business associations undertook to undermine public support for unions and liberalism in the early post–World War II years. Others have identified networks of conservative intellectuals, large firms, and think tanks that worked to similar ends as business sought to recoup its New Deal losses.[16] It was during this period that Lemuel Boulware, a General Electric vice president, fine-tuned the hard-bargaining strategy with unions that would become commonplace in the decades to come. His approach during the 1950s would have a lasting impact on GE's most famous employee—Ronald Reagan.[17] Clear from this line of scholarship is that few of the participants in labor–management relations would have described the period in terms of consensus. Even while large firms were bargaining with unions, they simultaneously funded or otherwise took part in numerous efforts to weaken and destabilize unions.

Moreover, whether one sides with the glass half-full or glass half-empty perspective on the capital–labor accord, most would agree that the industrial Midwest was the heart of this arrangement. It was the center of union strength where a mostly white working class reaped the benefits of unionized manufacturing work. This is where and when it was all supposed to work. But fights over labor rights nonetheless persisted and spilled over into the political arena. What then do we make of the considerable conflict in the Midwest where unions were strongest? How do we account for the campaigns over labor rights and the mobilization and influence of business and labor organizations, all of which varied significantly within the region? And what can it all tell us about the labor movement more generally?

In addressing these questions, I develop two general arguments in this book. First, the labor movement at its historical peak struggled to translate numbers into political influence and social acceptance in those states where union members were most densely populated. The stabilization of collective bargaining between large firms and industrial unions in this brief and, indeed, unusual historical period did not resolve this problem. The mixed showing by labor was due to both forces in their control—for instance, deep divisions within the labor movement—and forces beyond, including the limited organization and/or interest of some of the labor movement's most likely allies as well as considerable employer opposition. These limits come into focus when we bring the level of analysis down from a national accord between capital and labor or an alliance between the labor movement and the Democratic Party to the varied configurations of labor movements, allies, and opponents across states. Here we find dysfunctional union divisions, ambivalent political allies, and substantial employer opposition.

Understanding these limits is important. They diminished labor's electoral mobilizations and their society-wide influence. Labor not only had to contend with the vacuum of a nonunion Sunbelt that lured away jobs, but considerable opposition and limited political leverage where they were strongest. Even here at the center of union strength, a large share of industrial workers remained unorganized. The labor movement never solved many of the basic problems that slowed unions at their 1950s peak. The dearth of reliable allies and the limited responses to employer mobilization became a death knell as the economic environment worsened in the coming decades—a point I return to in the conclusion.[18]

Second, and related, no matter how big unions were, they needed a lot to go right in order to wield influence. Their grip in the industrial Midwest was often tenuous despite the heavy concentration of industry and union members. As I will show, there was still considerable rural and small business opposition and thus large shares of the population open to anti-union claims. Theories of social movements provide a useful analytical framework for understanding these conflicts by identifying the many moving parts typically necessary for movements—and, here, labor and their opponents—to impact the political process. They can help us make sense of the considerable variation in campaigns over labor rights and their effectiveness across otherwise similar highly unionized Midwestern states. Many of the key pieces activist groups typically need in order to succeed, including influential political allies and effective organizations, were not a given for labor at its peak but quite variable. This framework also helps us understand the political mobilization of business in these conflicts, something social movement scholars have mostly ignored until recently. Indeed, labor's effectiveness, and the effectiveness of most social movements for that matter, are best understood in interaction with their countermovement opposition. In using this framework, I assume that while economic structure poses very real constraints on the character of labor organization and conflict, it is not determinative. The past and future of the labor movement still rests on the ability of groups to mobilize workers and to develop, coordinate, and channel urgent political and economic demands. This is the stuff of social movements and contentious politics.[19]

Before outlining my analytical framework, readers might wonder if labor even qualifies as a social movement. After all, many unions had abandoned their militant origins, purged radicals from their ranks, and turned into large bureaucracies by the 1950s. I believe unions and their umbrella organizations, which include central labor bodies and labor federations like the AFL-CIO and their state and local affiliates—the organizations responsible for coordinating labor's political activities—fit most definitions of social movements. They involve collective challenges to authorities (employers and the state), and they frequently employ extra-institutional (strikes, rallies, protests) and institutional (lobbying, litigation, electioneering) tactics in these efforts. As labor scholar and organizer Jane McAlevey notes, the fact that many unions function as top-down bureaucracies does not make them all that unique in the social movement field. Many social movement organizations function in just this way, struggle with member engagement, or exhibit undemocratic tendencies. If anything, scholarship on a variety of non-labor social movements has documented the *increasing* formalization of social movement organizations and the routinization of activism in more recent decades. Staid, bureaucratic organization is hardly a disqualifier.[20]

More important than fitting any particular definition, social movement theories can help us understand the political contestation between labor and business. When locked in political conflicts, labor and business share with grassroots groups a need for leadership, allies, durable organizations, and the ability to frame issues in ways that resonate with broader audiences. Jill Quadagno's influential account of healthcare reform efforts in the twentieth century drew on social movement insights to understand the mobilization and effectiveness of a variety of healthcare stakeholders, including professional associations like the American Medical Association. Recent scholarship has pushed the boundaries of social movement theory to understand the mobilization of elites and firms and the rise of grassroots lobbying. Labor and business are different from most movement-countermovement pairs in some notable ways, as I describe later. Nevertheless, situating their conflicts in terms of political opportunities, competing organizations, and strategies helps make sense of the campaigns this book considers.[21]

Explaining Labor Rights Campaigns

A starting point is that social movements often need help from political allies or advantageous openings in the political system in order to accomplish their goals. Social movement scholars refer to these openings as political opportunities. Movements must also be perceptive enough to recognize and take advantage of political opportunities. This requires savvy organization. In the absence of opportunity, movements may press the issue by engaging in disruptive protest that is threatening to political elites, providing "negative inducements" for them to bargain. Alternatively, movements may seek out new partners and build coalitions that will carry more influence. As E. E. Schattschneider wrote long ago, it is the loser in a political conflict who calls for help. However, this matching of allies with capable social movement organizations is often fraught with trade-offs and conflict, not to mention that opponents are drawn to the same political arenas and often pursue similar competing strategies. This means that social movement influence is usually fleeting. This can be the case even for a group as resource-rich as unions in the 1950s.[22]

Throughout this book, I deploy social movement concepts of political opportunities, movement and countermovement organizations, and competing insider and outsider strategies as empirical variables to explain the outcomes of campaigns over labor rights. Understanding where and when movements will be impactful means gauging the relative mix of these three factors—factors that varied significantly even within a seemingly homogeneous region like the industrial Midwest so that routes to labor influence were highly localized. Labor succeeded when they secured powerful political allies, when they developed effective coalition strategies, and, importantly, when their opponents' organizations faltered.

I briefly unpack the three key pieces of the argument and how they map on to the labor movement in the 1950s; I save the more detailed discussion of social movement theory for the notes and concluding chapters.[23]

Political opportunities include a host of factors external to social movements that shape their likelihood of success, such as allies in government, ties with political parties and party leaders, popular support for movement causes, and points of access or leverage within states. In short, social movements need help from others in order to succeed. One of the most consistent findings from this literature is that movements need allies in government or a favorable partisan context to achieve their goals. For example, Edwin Amenta's political mediation argument suggests movements will *only* succeed with help from like-minded state actors. Unions, of course, bring to the table a number of resources that politicians find useful, increasing the likelihood of strong alliances. These include endorsements, campaign contributions, and the mobilization of union members and get-out-the-vote drives for elections. In the legislative process, unions lobby and provide useful information on policies. They may help to sway other interest groups and political actors and are available to politicians as an ally on a range of issues. These exchange relationships helped the post–New Deal labor movement become an important anchor of the Democratic Party nationally.[24]

Despite these ties, unions and their most likely political allies were disorganized in ways that often precluded strong relationships. As political scientist Taylor Dark observed, "[t]he Democratic Party has been viewed in profoundly erroneous terms as a monolithic and unitary actor that makes decisions *as a party*, rather than what it actually is: an undisciplined hodgepodge of individual politicians loosely united under a single label." Union–party relations thus varied wildly across states. Well into the twentieth century, large swaths of the country were characterized by patronage party systems based on the promise of jobs in government, state contracts, or leniency in regulation. This often worked to the detriment of labor or like-mined social movements. David Mayhew describes how patronage-oriented parties saw unions, particularly active ones, as competitors. In extreme cases, party bosses tried to keep some of the early CIO unions out of cities altogether. More typical by the 1950s was that unions were relegated to secondary roles in patronage-oriented Democratic Party coalitions. Without central roles in parties, individual union leaders often sought to cut their own deals with politicians and go their own way on endorsements, further limiting political coordination.[25]

The strength of *movement and countermovement organizations* is another piece shaping social movement effectiveness in the political process. Organizations do much of the mundane work necessary for activist campaigns to take off and thrive, including recruiting, staging events, and getting activists to attend. Scholars have identified a number of features that matter for political influence, including size, professionalization, and cohesiveness. No matter how big, unions and labor federations still had to put their resources to work in effective ways. Indeed, a common finding in the social movement literature is that size is *not* the most important organizational feature. Research on a variety of activist campaigns—from the southern civil rights movement to farmworkers in California to women's jury-rights activism—suggests some types of groups are better than others at having their "finger on the pulse" of the political environment and effectively putting their resources to work. Marshall Ganz refers to this ability to match strategy to the political environment as "strategic capacity." Movements that have leaders and members with diverse skills and experiences, including connections to other social movements, are more likely to have it and are better able to navigate complex political environments than are their more insular peers.[26]

State labor movements, and particularly the state labor federations charged with coordinating political activity, varied in the skills and experience they brought to the table, partly due to the industrial makeup of the state, partly to the presence of a dominant union, like the autoworkers, and partly to chance. Many state federations were insular organizations not inclined to work with individuals and organizations outside their immediate orbit. They also varied in their ability to compel affiliated unions and their members to mobilize on labor issues. National unions and labor federations could provide an infusion of expertise when state actors lacked them, but state politics was an afterthought for much, though not all, of the labor movement during the 1950s. Regional directors of large industrial unions commanded considerable resources, often dwarfing that of the state federations. Still, these resources were typically marshalled for legislative crises and big elections rather than the slow work of educating members and building a broader labor–liberal coalition.

The more basic and pressing organizational problem was that the labor movement was deeply divided between the older, conservative craft unions of the AFL and the newer, more progressive industrial unions of the CIO. The merger of the two federations in 1955 did not resolve this conflict. Historically, the power of craft unions relied on their ability to monopolize the labor market in a particular trade (e.g., carpentry, plumbing), not on the state. This meant they would organize only a small slice of workers in a given worksite. They were exclusive by nature. With few exceptions, they were racist and sexist organizations, sometimes limiting membership to a particular ethnic group or to relatives of existing members. By contrast, the CIO grew out of the industrial chaos and New Deal legislation of the 1930s. Led by shrewd unionists like John Lewis of the United Mine Workers (UMW) and Sidney Hillman of the Amalgamated Clothing Workers (ACW), the new industrial union movement sought to organize all workers in mass production industries regardless of skill or race. They literally banked their fortunes on the reelection of President Roosevelt in 1936. CIO unions were thus more inclusive and more political by nature, though this too varied significantly across CIO unions and between their leaders and union membership. While the aggressive organizing strategy and big gains of CIO unions in the 1930s and 1940s forced many AFL unions to change, the divergent outlooks of the two wings of the labor movement remained.[27]

After the formation of the AFL-CIO in 1955, rival state federations that had yet to merge sometimes refused to coordinate on legislative issues altogether and attacked each other in public. While labor and social movement scholarship has identified some benefits of conflict, it posed a significant challenge to labor's political mobilization. Joel Rogers summed up the decentralized and often disorganized character of the US labor movement, noting that "instead of being more than the sum of its parts . . . the American labor movement is usually less." While unions were big across the states of the industrial Midwest, their organizational capacity varied significantly.[28]

Political opportunities and the organizational makeup of state labor movements and employer-led countermovements shaped the range of *insider* and *outsider strategies* deployed in campaigns over labor rights. By insider, I mean working within formal political institutions (e.g., lobbying and electioneering). By outsider, I mean working outside of formal political institutions (e.g., community coalitions and outreach, strikes, and protest). The appeal of the insider route depended largely on whether labor's likely political allies were interested and/or organized enough to help. However, some state labor movements struggled to do anything other than insider work, even when political allies were few. Outsider strategies included labor militancy and protest but also the formation of broad coalitions with civil society groups that carried more weight than unions on their own. Gilbert Gall's research on right-to-work finds that for unions to be successful, they first had to develop a "public articulation of the labor movement's self-value to the community." This often meant forging alliances with non-labor groups that could make a better case for unions being in the public interest.[29]

Developing a public case for labor rights also meant changing how unions talked about labor rights. Scholarship on collective action frames considers the signifying work of social movements—that is, how they produce and maintain meaning for members, opponents, or other audiences. Research shows how framing is important for the political outcomes of social movements. Here, unions faced an uphill battle. Cedric de Leon's research demonstrates how collective action by workers came to be defined in terms of restraints on individual liberty as nineteenth-century employment relations were being rewritten in the context of slave emancipation. Rather than a historical artifact, this emergent "anti-labor democracy," hostile to collective labor rights altogether, has had considerable staying power and rhetorical appeal despite the interventions by the New Deal state in the 1930s.[30] Still, framing research suggests some potential inroads for labor. For example, credible claims that relate to real-world events and that are salient to the lived experiences of the target audience are more likely to resonate. The status of the frame-articulator also contributes to this frame resonance. Here, the claims of more highly regarded (often non-labor) individuals or organizations may be better received. Both business and labor sought out community allies at various times to bolster their respective positions in just this way, though this usually required far-sighted leadership and organizational stability, things labor often lacked.[31]

Figure 1.1 shows the basic scheme of how political opportunities, labor and countermovement organizations, and competing insider and outsider strategies shape campaigns over labor rights and labor's political influence more generally. Here I assume there are multiple potential pathways to campaign outcomes and do not give primacy to certain political opportunities over organizational features or vice versa, though groups typically need considerable strength in one or both areas to develop effective strategies and to counter employer influence. The essential point is that many of the key ingredients for social movement influence were not a given in the 1950s. The natural state of affairs for labor, even at the peak of its strength

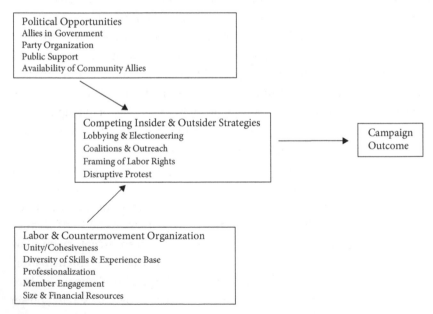

Figure 1.1 Opportunity, Organization, and Strategy in Labor Rights Campaigns

in the industrial Midwest, often militated *against* political influence. It was characterized by disorganized or even warring labor federations and/or disorganized or disinterested allies. This complicated everything from union member mobilization to coalition formation and framing to lobbying and electioneering. It left unions vulnerable to challenges from employer groups in the 1950s. It also made it harder for them to advance pro-labor efforts in seemingly favorable environments. Breaking away from this disorganized state to deploy their sizeable resources in effective ways required a push from far-sighted national unions or unusually resourceful local activists.[32]

A caveat is in order. The framework I employ assumes that the effectiveness of employer associations (e.g., state chambers of commerce and right-to-work groups) and labor organizations in political conflicts is shaped by similar forces. After all, these groups are drawn to the same political arenas and often forced to adopt similar competing strategies in what amounts to a "loosely-coupled tango."[33] Political opportunities, organization, and strategy are key to both sets of actors. Still, business and labor differ from most movement–countermovement pairs in important ways. Employers seek to sway labor's constituency in rank-and-file workers, and they exert significant control over workers' lives through the employment relationship. As Claus Offe and Helmut Wiesenthal observed, employers have an advantaged starting point due to their position in the class structure. Employers' goals are clear and accepted. Their communication with the state is built into the fabric of capitalism. In the language of social movement theory, political opportunities are less variable for business; they are often assumed. By contrast, labor is usually in catch-up mode. Labor has to organize workers with diverse interests and needs and compel them to act—or at least have the threat of their action—in order to counter employer influence.[34]

Employers, of course, are still vulnerable to public pressure and shifts in the political environment, as will be clear in the chapters that follow. Brand-visible firms have strong reasons *not* to stick their necks out and engage in controversial campaigns targeting labor.[35] However, the basic employer–union dynamic, stemming from employers' class position and their influence on union members through the employment relationship, persists no matter how big unions are. This means that political opportunities, organization, and strategy, while meaningful for both, do not play out in identical ways, as I will show.

Case Selection, Methods, and Plan of the Book

Why study labor politics in the Midwest in the 1950s? Why Indiana, Ohio, and Wisconsin in particular? The industrial Midwest was a bastion for unions in industries that were the backbone of the postwar American economy, including auto, steel, electrical products, and rubber. In the 1950s, the Midwest was an economic powerhouse and home to the nation's biggest corporations. The heavy manufacturing states around the Great Lakes accounted for more than half of the nation's manufacturing employment and were the center of union strength. Figure 1.2 plots union density for the industrial Midwest states of Illinois, Indiana, Michigan, Ohio, and Wisconsin relative to the other census regions.[36]

Indiana, Ohio, and Wisconsin are a critical part of the story of conflict over labor rights in the 1950s. These three states were interconnected sites of contention at a moment when labor rights were up for grabs in the region. Indiana stunned the labor movement by passing a right-to-work law in 1957, the northernmost industrial state to do so at the time. Prior to this, much of the labor movement had written off right-to-work as a southern phenomenon. The Indiana law changed this. The passage of right-to-work in a major industrial state where 40 percent of workers belonged to unions provided a

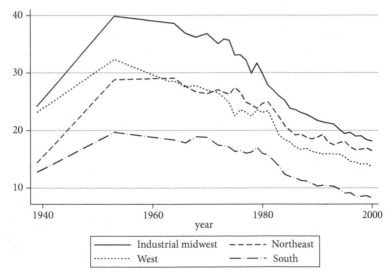

Figure 1.2 Union Density by Region, 1939–2000
Sources: Troy (1957); Hirsch and Macpherson (2003)

jolt of confidence for business leaders seeking restrictions on labor. So too did the sensational allegations of union corruption that began to emerge from the McClellan Committee in the US Senate. Established at the behest of congressional conservatives to investigate union corruption, the McClellan Committee employed over a hundred people, had offices in multiple cities, and took the testimony of more than fifteen hundred witnesses. Worse for labor, the committee broadcasted unions' dirty laundry to millions of Americans for the first time on television. Money flooded into state initiatives across the country. Right-to-work organizations popped up across the industrial Midwest. All eyes were on neighboring Ohio, where the state chamber of commerce launched a ballot initiative for right-to-work in 1958. This time, to the surprise of many, voters sided with labor in a landslide.

The perceived overreach by business activists proved disastrous for Republican candidates and temporarily tabled right-to-work legislation in the region. It also gave some life to long-dormant progressive labor policies. After more than a decade of building support for the idea, labor and Democratic Party activists helped Wisconsin become the first state to grant public employees the affirmative right to form and join unions in 1959. While the rise of public-sector collective bargaining is often associated with civil rights activism in the late 1960s and early 1970s, the first state law emerged when and where it did because of the fallout over labor rights in the Midwest. Public-sector unions had existed for decades. Large municipalities in the 1940s often bargained with public-sector unions with varying degrees of formality. Some states considered collective bargaining rights for public-sector workers even earlier. Yet openings for unions closed with the conservative resurgence at the end of the 1940s when several states passed restrictions on a host of private- and public-sector labor activities alike. It was only following the overreach by conservatives in 1958 that public-sector labor activists finally broke through in Wisconsin.[37]

I also consider the other big states in the region (more on them later), but Indiana, Ohio, and Wisconsin in particular capture much of the *action* in campaigns over labor rights in an important place and at an important historical moment. Relative to labor, the Indiana and Ohio campaigns are defensive, fighting off right-to-work legislation, while the Wisconsin campaign is offensive, pushing for new collective bargaining rights. All three are connected in this late 1950s employer pushback against unions (more on this in chapter 2). There are certainly other ways to gauge the strength of the labor movement, including union organizing or striking, but legislative campaigns provide an important opportunity to observe the political mobilization and effectiveness of labor and their opponents. No matter what, unions will inevitably encounter opposition. They will be forced to make a case for themselves to the state and to seek public support in the process. It is therefore useful beyond these particular cases and this particular period to understand what business and labor organizations do when put to the test, when they are forced to make a case for or against labor rights.

Moreover, the issues at hand—right-to-work and public-sector collective bargaining rights—were and remain highly significant. Right-to-work creates a free-rider problem for unions. After winning a representation election, unions are required to collectively bargain on behalf of all workers covered by the contract, but they cannot compel them to join and pay dues. It weakens unions at the bargaining table and in politics. It also provides an important signal of a pro-business environment with little resistance from labor or other like-minded social movements. Public-sector collective bargaining rights were central to the only significant growth for the labor movement in the second half of the twentieth century. Research shows that both policies significantly affect union density. Finally, just proposing any kind of restrictive labor policy requires unions to put up resources in opposition, something contemporary anti-labor forces understand well.[38]

Table 1.1 provides some context on the economic, social, and political characteristics of the three campaign states and their two large industrial neighbors in Illinois and Michigan. Together, these states comprise the East North Central census subregion and heart of the industrial Midwest. Before each case study, I detail the political opportunities and status of the labor movement and its opposition in that given state. As a general overview here, there are some similarities worth noting. In the 1950s, all of the states were characterized by heavy manufacturing employment and high union density, each well above the national average. Each state was also marked by a mostly white working class.[39] Despite the concentration of unions and heavy industry, the Midwest was more or less Republican dominated, particularly when it came to state politics. The more liberal unions of the CIO were often met by considerable local and small business opposition on both ideological and economic grounds. The region still had a sizeable rural farm population whose outlook was more insular. It is perhaps not surprising that the region was a hotbed for the 1920s Ku

Table 1.1 Cases and Context: The Industrial Midwest in the 1950s

	Indiana	Ohio	Wisconsin	Illinois	Michigan
Campaign outcome (1= pro-labor)	0	1	1	—	—
Labor and Industrial Composition					
Union density in 1953	40	38	38.3	39.7	43.3
Dominant labor federation (year of merger)	CIO (1957)	CIO (1958)	AFL (1958)	AFL (1958)*	CIO (1958)
% Employed in manufacturing in 1954	44.0	43.5	40.9	37.0	46.0
% Employed in public sector in 1954	11.4	11.1	11.5	10.2	10.4
Social and Political Organization					
% Black in 1950	4.4	6.5	0.8	7.4	6.9
% Foreign-born in 1950	2.5	5.6	6.3	9.1	9.5
% Rural farm population	17	10.7	21.1	8.8	10.9
% Voting for Eisenhower in 1956	59.9	61.1	61.6	59.52	55.63
% Republican legislature (1950s average)	0.63	0.64	0.69	0.58	0.64
Patronage party organization	Yes	Yes	No	Yes	No

*Chicago Federation of Labor does not join the state AFL-CIO until 1962.

Notes: Indiana passed right-to-work in 1957 and repealed the law in 1965, only to pass it again in 2012 (see chapters 3 and 6). Labor and industrial composition data are from Troy (1957) and *Statistical Abstract of the United States*, various years. Demographic data are from the US Bureau of the Census (1975). Political data from congressional quarterly Voting and Elections Collection, and Jordan and Grossmann (2016).

Klux Klan, which organized by stoking fears about moral decay and social disorder brought by waves of immigration and economic change.[40]
While Wisconsin had the most celebrated progressive legacy, it settled on
a business-dominated Republican course in the 1940s and, by the 1950s,
had become better known for the militant anti-communism of Senator
Joseph McCarthy.[41]

Unions' grip on the industrial Midwest therefore was not entirely secure. Beyond their sheer size and resources, they still needed a lot to go
right in order to impact the political process. My focus in the case studies is
on these key pieces—political opportunities, labor and countermovement
organizations, and their competing insider and outsider strategies—and
how they influenced campaigns over labor rights. Here, there are notable
differences, from the particular mix of AFL and CIO unions to the organization of political parties and the availability of allies. After assessing the
campaigns in Indiana, Ohio, and Wisconsin, I return to the state of right-
to-work and public-sector bargaining in the region more generally and
consider labor relations and politics in Illinois and Michigan. Doing so
provides a better understanding of the labor relations of the period. It also
allows us to see if the campaign states were atypical in any way.[42]

I draw on a wide range of archival materials to construct historical
narratives of each campaign. These materials include organizational
records and correspondence of labor and business groups, outreach and
promotional materials generated by these actors, their public testimony,
governors' records, and oral histories of political representatives and
participants in the campaigns. Like any methodological strategy, one that
relies heavily on archival materials poses certain challenges. Archival data
in particular are prone to selection bias in that the records of larger, more
resourceful organizations are more likely to be stored in the first place, and
the inclusion of particular materials is often done in nonrandom ways.
Fortunately, for this case I examine the often very public mobilization of
large and resourceful organizations. The public officials involved in these
conflicts typically had at least some reporting requirements. While the
possibility of selection bias cannot be eliminated completely, it is less of a
concern for this study. I supplement these primary materials with media
produced by key actors (labor and trade press) and mainstream news coverage of the events, secondary histories, interviews with contemporary
practitioners and observers, and a host of publicly available data on labor,
business, and politics in the mid-twentieth century.[43]

Plan of the Book

Chapter 2 sets the stage for the case studies of labor rights campaigns. I provide a sketch of labor relations during the 1950s, noting where the imagery of the capital–labor accord holds and where it falls short. I show how using the 1950s as a critical reference point when explaining union decline tends to obscure key vulnerabilities that labor has long exhibited, well before the fallout in manufacturing and the rise of economic globalization. Gains workers accrued through collective bargaining were exceptional in many ways, though union strength was confined to a relatively narrow geographic and industrial space. Even here, in the industrial Midwest, there were intense struggles over the legitimacy of unions. This came to a head at the end of the decade when employers made a concerted push for right-to-work.

The campaigns considered in chapters 3–5 underscore my first general argument by showing how labor divisions, disinterest or disorganization among likely allies, and employer opposition complicated the transfer of numbers into political influence at labor's peak. In chapters 3 and 4, I examine campaigns for right-to-work laws in Indiana and Ohio at the end of the decade. Each shows far-reaching business mobilization to curb union strength—from work in the community to their posture at the bargaining table to the legislative process. In Indiana, union efforts to fight off right-to-work were hobbled by dysfunctional infighting and sophisticated employer efforts to isolate unions from community partners. The passage of right-to-work in Indiana sent shock waves throughout the labor movement and brought more national union involvement in state politics, at least temporarily. Ohio unions reversed the right-to-work outcome the following year thanks in part to assistance from the national labor movement, which emphasized building coalitions with respected civil society partners. In this case, it was Ohio business leaders who were disconnected from their likely allies.

Chapter 5 traces the development of a new path in public-sector collective bargaining rights in Wisconsin. The affirmative case for public-sector rights that Wisconsin unions waged lacked the fanfare of the Indiana and Ohio campaigns, though it was clearly shaped by them. It was after more than a decade of public-sector advocates organizing and introducing bills in the legislature and after the overreach of business activists on right-to-work in the region that dissension within the Republican Party and between party leaders and business circles provided the opening activists needed. The insider route that public-sector union activists pursued did not involve a wide-ranging co-alition, many strikes, or much protest. Instead, it hinged on the slow culti-vation of key political allies. Working with a revitalized Democratic Party, public-sector union advocates sidestepped legislative restrictions on unions and gained new rights for public-sector workers in 1959.

The final two chapters expand the geographic and temporal focus to consider how these processes played out across other key Midwestern states and connect to labor's current struggles. In chapter 6, I take up the state of right-to-work and public-sector collective bargaining rights and assess their development in the region and elsewhere in the two decades following the 1950s conflicts. I then turn to labor politics in Michigan and Illinois in particular. While each of the case studies highlights some of the many moving parts necessary for labor to impact the political process, chapter 6 puts these factors in comparative perspective. This underscores the second general argument, informed by social movement theory, on the necessary pieces for union influence. I identify multiple context-contingent routes to labor success, one relying more on political oppor-tunities and one on outsider coalitions. Both required a break away from the routine of divided labor federations and disinterested political allies. While there are some notable differences within the region, such as the impressive labor–liberal coalition in Michigan, it is marked mostly by the disorganization of labor and its allies. Fortunately for labor, employers also struggled with coordination and securing support from key polit-ical allies. Yet, even after business opposition temporarily receded in the 1960s, the disorganization of labor and its allies slowed the growth of public-sector collective barging rights in the region.

I conclude in chapter 7 by reviewing the main findings of the book and consider how the struggles of the 1950s map onto challenges to union legitimacy today. I argue that the 1950s conflicts over labor rights were more than an interesting side story. Labor never completely con-quered the Midwest, where most union members resided during these years, not to mention the Sunbelt, where most future economic growth would occur. This limited union influence at its peak. Indeed, labor had to scrap it out when times were good. Many of the vulnerabilities unions exhibited then—weak or nonexistent ties to groups outside of the labor movement, ambivalent political allies, inadequate responses to employer mobilization—were magnified in the coming decades, beginning with the economic downturns in the 1970s and continuing to the present day.

Despite the hollowing out of the industrial Midwest, contemporary fights over union rights there still bear many of the same features of the 1950s. While state labor movements generally developed more sophisticated political operations and formed a closer relationship with Democrats following the conflicts in the 1950s, enduring labor–community coalitions have proven elusive. They are needed now more than ever.

2

The Capital–Labor Accord in Action

Ask someone to describe the 1950s. If they can conjure up anything, it might center on idyllic suburbs, or the boredom and social conformity of the decade compared to the 1960s, or maybe something out of the popular sitcom *Leave It to Beaver*, which debuted in 1957. If you were to ask a social scientist to describe the 1950s, they would be a bit more skeptical and less nostalgic, though they too would probably emphasize consensus. Save for a burgeoning civil rights struggle in the South, the decade is often seen as the quiet one, sandwiched between the ravages of the Great Depression and two world wars on one side and the protest cycle of the long 1960s on the other. It is the peak of what labor scholars have described as the capital–labor accord. This loose arrangement between unions and large firms, marked by a period of relative labor peace, helped promote stable collective bargaining relationships and produced sizeable gains for ordinary workers.[1]

Like social life generally, the labor relations of the period were more contentious in practice. Indeed, any accord between capital and labor was often lost on the key players. As the labor movement settled on a more conservative path, the business community became more strident in its opposition to unions. The decade is bookended by enormous labor conflicts in the steel industry, marked by the unsuccessful seizure of steel plants by President Truman in 1952 and the biggest strike in US history launched by the United Steelworkers in 1959. One common thread is that businesses of various size still sought to slow unions where they could, whether or not they participated in collective bargaining.

This chapter provides a sketch of labor relations in the 1950s and sets the stage for the case studies in chapters 3–5. I begin by describing common uses of the capital–labor accord framework, where it was most likely to hold, and what it gets right and wrong about the labor relations of the period. I show that while the gains workers accrued through collective bargaining were exceptional in many ways, union strength was confined to a relatively narrow geographic and industrial space. Even here, as in the industrial Midwest, there were intense struggles over the legitimacy of unions. This came to a

Heartland Blues. Marc Dixon, Oxford University Press (2020). © Oxford University Press.
DOI: 10.1093/oso/9780190917036.001.0001.

head at the end of the decade when employers pushed for right-to-work. The receptiveness of communities and politicians to competing claims over labor rights in these struggles shows that unions were often in a tenuous position. Indeed, many of the key forces argued to shape social movement influence that I outlined in chapter 1—political allies, strong organization, and effective strategy—proved to be a struggle for labor at the peak of its powers.

Labor Relations in the 1950s

Cooperation between big business and organized labor following World War II is presented as a key piece of the regulated capitalism that dominated much of the 1950s and 1960s, the so-called golden age of industrial capitalism and the peak of the capital–labor accord. The labor movement was indeed big by the 1950s. Unions represented a third of all workers. As economic historian David Kotz argues, the acceptance of collective bargaining by many large firms alongside Keynesian macroeconomic policies and a budding welfare state combined to produce relatively stable labor relations, economic growth, and significant profits. The economic gains were unusually widely distributed. The income of the median worker doubled in the two decades following the war. Home ownership soared. And unemployment remained low for the most part. There were opponents to regulated capitalism, particularly small firms with razor-thin margins who were unable to pass on higher costs to consumers. Yet they were too weak, relative to both big business and labor, to prevent its consolidation in the immediate postwar period.[2]

Unions mattered in ways that are hard to imagine today. Major collective bargaining agreements in the three decades after World War II often set the pattern for industry-wide wage increases extending well beyond unionized workers. More, unions helped to make health insurance, pensions, and supplemental unemployment benefits a reality for average workers. Unions curbed inequality by promoting "norms of equity," not just at the bargaining table but culturally and politically as well. None of these accomplishments were easy or free of contention. Striking remained high throughout the postwar period. There were more than 250 major strikes involving 1,000 workers or more annually during the 1950s (compared to 10–20 today). But unions achieved sizeable gains for their members and the working and middle classes more generally. Considering just the economic gains, the working class has not experienced anything like this before or after.[3]

Most posit that this loose arrangement between capital and labor began shortly after World War II and lasted until the economic crises of the early 1970s. Deteriorating economic conditions, increased global competition, and the demands posed by a host of new social movements all contributed to a break in the corporate side of this arrangement. According to Mark Mizruchi's influential account of the corporate elite over the last century, big business in the postwar era was mostly pragmatic and learned how to live with unions. This held until the economic crises of the 1970s, when firms sought to shed expensive labor contracts, became more militant in resisting unions in the workplace, and collectively mobilized against labor law reform in Congress.[4]

Whether it all ended with the 1973 oil crisis or the coordinated push-back against proposed labor reforms later in the decade, all agree that the 1950s and 1960s were the high-water mark of the accord. Yet it was only in the 1980s—after steep declines in union membership became apparent— that labor activists and sympathetic scholars began to describe the postwar period as a capital–labor accord. Some of the accord literature was from an activist perspective. For example, in their 1989 book, Service Employees International Union leaders John Sweeney and Karen Nussbaum decried the breaking of a "social contract" between business and labor, one which they argue began with the labor laws of the 1930s. Whereas business once accepted unions and saw the well-being of the workforce as an important objective, Sweeney and Nussbaum contend that corporate leaders had all but abandoned this commitment by the 1970s and 1980s.[5]

Writing in 1983, left-leaning economists Samuel Bowles, David Gordon, and Thomas Weisskopf described the two-to-three decades following World War II as an accord involving a set of implicit trade-offs between big business and unions. This imagery was not always a positive one for unions, no matter how impressive the economic gains. Unions functioned in part as an agent of labor discipline; they would not challenge managerial prerogatives over the organization of work and would ensure workers did not strike between contracts. Unions, of course, still sought to establish and maintain formal work rules as a safeguard against expanding managerial authority, but they channeled worker militancy and grievances into predictable and routinized forms. In return, large firms mostly accepted unions instead of fighting them and rewarded workers with rising incomes made possible through produc-tivity gains.[6]

While most of the accord references focus first on collective bargaining, there was a social and political foundation upholding it. Unions, it is argued, were accepted as legitimate pillars of working life by business, workers, and the state. Unions and blue-collar workers were an important part of a Democratic voting bloc, often in an uneasy alliance with liberals, intellectuals, and increasingly African Americans. This coalition helped preserve many of the gains of the New Deal. Labor, and especially the new AFL-CIO, lobbied the Democratic Party to become more progressive on labor issues. Considering the influence of the New Deal and World War II state on the development of industrial unions and the revival of the labor movement more generally, it is not surprising that this political strategy focused heavily on national elections and lobbying congress, all of it centered in Washington, DC, and headed by the AFL-CIO's Committee on Political Education (COPE).[7]

The trajectory of the labor movement during the 1950s fits with the narrative of the accord in at least two important ways. First, most unions had abandoned any hint of their prior radicalism and appeared willing to bargain with business. By the late 1940s when political columnist and pollster Samuel Lubell returned to a United Auto Workers (UAW) local he first visited eight years earlier, he noticed that the photos of strikes and clashes with police, or any evidence of insurgency for that matter, had come down in favor of idyllic snapshots of union social outings and sporting events. "The labor dynamo has slowed down," Lubell concluded. This opinion was shared by many on the political left. C. Wright Mills, who chronicled the leaders of the CIO in his 1948 book *The New Men of Power*, soon gave up on labor as any kind of progressive social movement.[8]

Second, many large firms did come around to accept if not embrace collective bargaining after World War II. The Committee for Economic Development (CED) provided an important channel through which business leaders reached consensus on collective bargaining. Formed to deal with postwar reconversion, the CED Board of Trustees was a "who's who" of big firms, including the likes of Ford, General Electric, Coca Cola, and B. F. Goodrich. By 1947, the CED offered policy positions not to thwart collective bargaining, but to streamline it and make it less disruptive to business. Emblematic of this approach was the generous five-year collective bargaining contract between General Motors (GM) and the UAW in 1950. Writing in *Fortune* magazine, Daniel Bell dubbed it the "Treaty of Detroit," noting that while GM made a sizeable commitment on its end, "it got a bargain" in the return of labor peace.[9]

Given the successes of unions in the mid-twentieth century and labor's precipitous fall in the decades to come, it is no wonder that scholars often seek to understand contemporary union struggles in relation to the heyday of union strength. And the economic gains cannot be ignored. Yet this historical comparison tends to both obscure some of labor's weaknesses during the 1950s and overestimate the willingness of employers to go along with this loose arrangement. It also misses the strong feelings individuals held about unions, including the deep hostility held by many. I take up these issues throughout the rest of this chapter, first outlining the geographic scope of the accord and the centrality of the industrial Midwest. I then turn to continued business resistance to unionism during the 1950s, including in the industrial heartland.

Limits to Union Power

Where did the accord hold at the peak of industrial unionism in the 1950s? As I describe later, opportunities for a robust union movement in the South closed quickly in the immediate postwar period, after which many union leaders gave up on the region, precluding any large-scale coalition with a budding civil rights movement. In terms of industry, some analysts distinguish between unionized and nonunionized sectors in the postwar era. For example, Beth Rubin's analysis of striking and wages following World War II finds significant differences between core unionized industrial sectors— mining, manufacturing, construction, transportation, communication, and public utilities—and the nonunion mostly service sector. Only in the core unionized sectors was striking a fairly stable and routinized mechanism of industrial action ensuring wage gains. Bruce Nissen offers a more nuanced view, noting how the accord was highly uneven across and within major industrial sectors. The accord rested in part on the ability of strong individual unions to dominate the field. Auto and steel come closest to this characterization. Where unions were divided (electrical products) or failed to gain a strong foothold (chemicals), employers were more strident in their resistance. Midsize manufacturers and family-owned firms were even less inclined to work with unions and were often at the front of campaigns to limit union influence.[10]

Table 2.1 lists the states for where the accord was most likely to hold using three different rankings moving from least to most stringent criteria. The first two include the top fifteen states according to the percentage of non-agricultural workers in the core unionized industry sectors and then the percentage of nonagricultural workers just in auto and steel production as of the mid-1950s. For the third ranking, I include those states that are in the top fifteen for both employment rankings *and* for the percent of workers unionized. Three southern states appear on the employment rankings, but none of them are highly unionized and each was stridently anti-union by the 1950s. The remaining states appearing on both lists and which have high percentages of workers belonging to unions are tightly clustered in the upper Midwest and Mid-Atlantic and include the focal states in this study. By these metrics, the accord was confined to a relatively narrow geographic and industrial space. As the following chapters show, unions' grip was put to the test in these strongholds.

Table 2.1 The Reach of the Capital–Labor Accord in the 1950s

State Rank	Core Industry Employment	Auto & Steel Employment	State in Top 15 for Core Industry, Auto & Steel, and Unionization (Union Density in Parentheses)	
1	Connecticut	Michigan	West Virginia	(44.1)
2	Michigan	Indiana	Michigan	(43.3)
3	West Virginia	Ohio	Indiana	(40)
4	New Jersey	Connecticut	Pennsylvania	(39.9)
5	Delaware	Kansas	Wisconsin	(38.3)
6	Pennsylvania	Maryland	Ohio	(38)
7	Ohio	Pennsylvania	New Jersey	(35.2)
8	Indiana	California		
9	New Hampshire	Washington		
10	Rhode Island	Alabama		
11	South Carolina	Wisconsin		
12	North Carolina	Arizona		
13	Wisconsin	New Jersey		
14	Maine	Missouri		
15	Illinois	West Virginia		

Sources: Statistical Abstract of the US (1955); US Census of Manufactures (1954); Troy (1957).

The second limit to the accord was in the willingness of firms to go along with this arrangement and the ability of unions to establish themselves as legitimate partners. While General Motors and other large firms more or less signed on to the Treaty of Detroit and bargained with unions, they were simultaneously funding a variety of new conservative organizations that sought to undermine the labor movement. Dozens of national conservative organizations emerged during the decade to curb unions, the welfare state, and the ideas on which they rested. The 1950s also witnessed the beginning of the modern anti-union consultant industry where lawyers and consultants replaced the Pinkertons of old.[11] Firms themselves went on the offensive, holding town hall meetings, in-plant educational sessions, and waging larger political campaigns to sway workers and communities away from unions and the dangers of collectivism. The number of Unfair Labor Practice charges (ULPs) filed by unions against firms doubled in the late 1950s.[12]

Many of the issues at stake in the 1950s had lingered since the explosion of industrial unionism during the Great Depression. Following the passage of the Wagner Act in 1935, which granted workers the right to form and join unions and to collectively bargain with their employers, many businesses still held firm in their resistance, assuming that the law would be overturned like the National Recovery Act before it. When the Wagner Act was upheld by the Supreme Court in 1937, employers were forced to the table, but many questions remained. The act excluded large groups of workers—supervisors, domestic and agricultural workers, public employees—and said little about how unions could regulate their own organizations or even collect dues. Despite the spectacular sit-down strikes and the rapid organization of basic industry in 1937, the new industrial unions were on the verge of bankruptcy and had little leverage to bargain when the economy turned sour again in 1938. Employers were in no mood to bargain. Nearly all business segments large and small favored the repeal or significant modification of the Wagner Act.[13]

State backing and a tight wartime labor market provided a critical boost to the union movement in the 1940s, but it did not resolve these basic issues. Unemployment dropped to a miniscule 1.3 percent in 1943. Yet, just as favorable rulings from the National War Labor Board provided the new industrial unions a measure of stability by requiring workers in defense industries to remain in their union and pay dues for the length of the contract (usually a year at that point), business interests, with few immediate options for overhauling the Wagner Act, took their case to state legislatures. In the

South, new political organizations championed right-to-work laws, which forbid the union shop and significantly weakened unions. The Christian American Association out of Houston was the first in the nation to champion right-to-work as a full-blown political slogan. Led by Vance Muse, a former oil lobbyist and consummate salesman, the organization stood out in a crowded field for its fiery rhetoric against the New Deal, Roosevelt, and especially labor. Writing in the 1940s, political scientist Manning Dauer identified them as one of the "many types of movements which openly or covertly depart from the democratic condition." Muse became intrigued by the use of the right-to-work term in a 1941 Labor Day editorial in the *Dallas Morning News* that called for an open-shop amendment to the constitution. After traveling to Dallas and consulting with the editor, Muse was encouraged to use and promote the idea widely. It became their primary cause.[14]

The big postwar southern union organizing drives beginning in 1946, launched first by the CIO and then followed by the rival AFL, failed to give unions a foothold in the region. The CIO first tried to assuage the fears of southern employers on multiple fronts. They poured resources into organizing white textile workers over black and interracial workforces. The CIO completely separated their union organizing and political activities. They hired a slew of conservative southern organizers. None of this worked. Several states quickly passed right-to-work laws in response to the drives. Southern employers pushed back with a viscous campaign of race and red-baiting and outright violence. By the early 1950s, unions had fewer members in the South than when the organizing drives began. Despite a five-fold gain in membership since the Depression, unions had not established any kind of national, far-reaching movement.

On the heels of the massive postwar strike wave, when more than one million workers went on strike, Republicans ran on the slogan "Had Enough?" and retook control of Congress. The new Congress passed the Taft-Hartley Act over President Truman's veto in June 1947. Among other things, the new law established unfair labor practices on the part of unions, it outlawed secondary boycotts, it required labor leaders to take an anti-communist affidavit, and it affirmed the rights of states to pass and enforce right-to-work laws. The law enraged union leaders. John L. Lewis, the larger than life president of the UMW, saw it as "the first ugly, savage thrust of fascism in America." Incensed that employers did not have to sign an anti-communist affidavit, Lewis refused.[15]

While unions struggled to regroup and undo key portions of the act, states had already gone further. Many of the big industrial unions were indifferent or just unaware of the extent of the damage. In May 1947, CIO general counsel Lee Pressman had to warn his organization's executive board of the damage mounting in the states: "I don't know whether the members of the Board recognize it, but in about 12 or 13 states, in addition to this Federal Congress, legislation has already been enacted. . . . I am afraid that not too serious efforts were made in the various states to combat state legislation." He was right. Fourteen states passed right-to-work prior to Congress affirming states' rights to do so in section 14(b) of the Taft-Hartley Act. Many states did more. Texas passed nine different restrictions on labor unions in 1947, from an anti-dues check-off law to measures outlawing mass-picketing to a prohibition of public employee unionism, something neither the Wagner Act nor Taft-Hartley addressed. Indeed, just as some states began to consider legal recognition of public-sector unions, the conservative pushback that spread across the country closed off this possibility for another decade.[16]

Following the political setbacks of 1947 and the dawning of Cold War politics, the communist issue exploded within the CIO. Many of the unions at the "center" and "right" of the federation, including the UAW and CIO president Philip Murray's own United Steel Workers began raiding the membership of allegedly communist-dominated unions. This was formalized in the purges of 1949–1950 when the CIO expelled eleven of its own member unions for being under communist control. Murray claimed at the 1950 CIO convention that the purging of communists made the organization more effective and militant. But this was not the case. As Judith Stepan Norris and Maurice Zeitlin's work documents, the purge rid the CIO of those elements "that were most dynamic, egalitarian, democratic, class-conscious, and advanced on issues of women rights and interracial solidarity." Unions mostly abandoned southern organizing during these years and the prospects for any civil rights–labor fusion were lost for another two decades.[17]

Unions were also becoming increasingly bureaucratic. For example, the UAW's staff tripled between 1949 and 1970, a period when there were no meaningful gains in the union's membership. The UAW was not alone. Part of the expansion in union staffing was due to increasingly complex contract negotiations where unions were responsible for negotiating health coverage and insurance plans. White-collar staff were critical for collective bargaining, but this emphasis sapped much of the "movement" out of labor. Dan Clawson describes union leaders of the period as needing to be some "combination of informal social workers, employment lawyers, and old-time machine politicians." Not on the list was labor activist. Unions were weakened at the grassroots level and far less ambitious at the top as they sought to negotiate with business at the dawn of the 1950s. Business was not convinced.[18]

Business Resistance to Unionism in the 1950s

The anti-labor mobilization in the 1950s was not confined to likes of shadowy far-right characters like Vance Muse. To be sure, militant anti-communists like Robert Welch and the John Birch Society he formed in Indianapolis at the end of the decade were staunch opponents. So, too, were Old Right isolationists like former Notre Dame dean Clarence Manion, who used his popular radio forum in the Midwest to attack labor and New Deal liberalism. But the conservative anti-labor activists of the 1950s ranged from family-owned though still large Midwestern firms like bathroom appliance manufacturer Kohler to brand-name General Electric and its militantly antiunion vice president Lemuel Boulware. "Boulwarism" became known in industrial relations circles for the hardline bargaining with unions that he pioneered at GE during the 1950s.

Boulware, burned by union gains in the 1940s, urged business leaders to do more to reverse the inroads labor had made with workers and communities. Writing in the *Journal of Education and Sociology* in 1953, he argued that business provided good jobs and a healthy tax base, but it needed fair treatment in return: "[I]n too many communities . . . it is considered by public servants in anything approaching 'labor trouble' that it is good politics to protect even flagrant law *breakers* in their abuses of the persons and property of peaceful and law-*abiding* citizens" (emphasis in original). To reverse the tide, Boulware urged business leaders to become more organized and involved in politics, otherwise the status quo of the "skilled [labor] demagogue" outflanking the "unskilled businessman" would continue. Boulware's message was not just for executives. His in-house educational programs reached 190,000 employees and he encouraged other firms to engage in a similar brand of community and political outreach to sway employees away from labor's positions on the economy and economic fairness. By the end of the 1950s, several firms followed his lead in training management-level employees to run for office, map out precincts, and canvass door to door.[19]

Historian Kim Phillips-Fein shows how many large firms beyond GE provided critical support to a host of new conservative organizations and think tanks tackling labor issues in the 1950s. These included the American Enterprise Association (later Institute), formed in 1943 and which came to flourish during the 1950s under the leadership of General Dynamics executive Allen Marshall; the smaller Foundation for Economic Education headed by Leonard Read and established with help from the B. F. Goodrich Company; and the extensive community outreach programs of the National Association of Manufacturers (NAM). William F. Buckley founded the *National Review* in 1955. Drawing much of its support from textile manufacturer and fellow Yale alum Roger Milliken, the magazine focused heavily on union malfeasance and the dangerous political ambitions of the labor movement in its early years. All of these organizations had wide support in the business community. Several of the CED member firms who had reluctantly come around to collective bargaining after the war had sought out other means to undermine unions by the mid-1950s.[20]

Some of the legal strategies slowing unions today likewise began to take shape in the 1950s. Sylvester Petro, a steelworker from the South Side of Chicago turned law professor and anti-union strategist, helped shape the libertarian critique of unions that the New Right would ultimately embrace. In 1957, he published his critique of the New Deal Labor regime in *The Labor Policy of the Free Society*. Through this and other works as a law professor at New York University and later Wake Forest, Petro contended that union influence was political in its origins. Government backing of compulsory unionism through the union shop and its mandate for employers to collectively bargain, he argued, impinged upon freedom of association. His work won him praise from the Wisconsin bathroom appliance manufacturer Kohler, who sought him out to provide expert analysis and eventually a hard-hitting book on union and government overreach in the long and bitter UAW strike there. Petro was invited to testify before the McClellan Committee on union corruption in the Senate in 1959. The culmination of his work, however, would take another two decades when he argued before the Supreme Court in *Abood v. Detroit Board of Education* that all public-sector labor union activity was inherently political. This made any requirement of union dues or even a representation fee to support routine collective bargaining activities a violation of workers' First Amendment rights. Though the court did not embrace Petro's logic on representation fees in 1977, Petro's ideas came back around and were central to the establishment of a national right-to-work law in public-sector employment in *Janus v. AFSCME* in 2018.[21]

The merger of the AFL and the CIO in 1955 was seen by critics on the left as locking the labor movement on a conservative path. Three years earlier, William Green and Philip Murray, the leaders of the rival federations, died within a span of weeks. New leadership eased some of the old grudges and paved the way for reconciliation. The AFL was almost twice the size of the CIO at the time of the merger, allowing for George Meany to take the reins of the new federation instead of the more ambitious and progressive Walter Reuther of the UAW, who would head the new federation's Industrial Union Department (IUD). Meany's AFL-CIO was a forceful advocate for liberal policies, but it eschewed militancy and was emblematic of what critical scholars later termed "business unionism," where unions function mostly as an insurance policy for workers.[22]

Meany outlined his more conciliatory approach in a speech to the National Association of Manufacturers (NAM) in December 1955: "I believe in the free enterprise system completely," he assured the audience of business executives. "I believe in return on capital investment. I believe in management's right to manage. . . . It is merely for us to disagree, if you please, as to what share the worker gets, what share management gets."[23] Business leaders undoubtedly preferred Meany to Reuther. Yet, as Elizabeth Fones Wolf shows, most still feared the consolidated federation, thinking it would prompt renewed organizing drives, militancy, and greater power in politics and at the bargaining table. The Chamber of Commerce magazine, *Nation's Business*, ran a series of articles in 1955 on the proposed merger and its likely effects, replete with photos of new and lavish union headquarters in Washington, DC, as evidence of labor's impending takeover of government. Their claim that the country was heading toward a "labor government" was not seen as particularly outlandish or part of some conspiracy hatched by the far right. A chamber of commerce official in Wisconsin captured this fear when lobbying against the prospect of public-sector unions, claiming the new federation is "nearly a third party" that could mean "the end of our capitalist system."[24]

Business angst was not entirely unfounded. At the peak of labor-liberal influence in the mid-twentieth century, unions were a highly influential lobby in Congress. The efforts of labor's new political arm COPE were impressive. Union households tended to vote Democratic in congressional and presidential elections. In return, the labor movement headed by the AFL-CIO became an important anchor of the Democratic Party nationally. Unions were successful in making the northern wing of the party pro-worker even if they could not prod them to undo Taft-Hartley. Still, the labor movement business feared was in many ways a Washington affair. The national AFL-CIO and its considerable resources did not eliminate the decentralized and often disorganized character of union political programs—or parties for that matter. Many state labor federations remained divided following the merger of the AFL and CIO, as we will see. Some refused to coordinate on political activities, and their disputes were often messy and public, a point not lost on employers. As political scientist Steven Amberg noted on the limits of union political action during these years, coordination between "a decentralized labor movement and a decentralized party proved complex." State COPEs were fairly autonomous and varied considerably in effectiveness and the level of buy-in among local unions. There was good reason for the AFL-CIO to focus on Congress, but this emphasis meant that state politics was often an afterthought. This at a time when the NAM and national Chamber of Commerce were increasingly turning to highly unionized states for labor reforms.[25]

Meany and NAM president Charles Sligh had engaged in private talks to find common ground in 1955. These broke down as the NAM embarked on a new public relations campaign to expose the abuses of now "Big Labor." New organizations targeting labor stepped up alongside the NAM and the Chamber of Commerce. The National Right-to-Work Committee (NRTWC), headed by former congressman and cosponsor of the Taft-Hartley Act, Fred Hartley, opened shop in 1955. Film director and labor antagonist Cecil DeMille and his foundation likewise targeted unions during the 1950s, often soliciting employers for examples of labor abuses to include in their expanding promotional materials and political campaigns.[26]

There was ample material for business activists to draw from in the 1950s. Some of it came from explosive labor conflicts in the Midwest, the very center of the accord. In Newcastle, Indiana, in 1955, a gun fight broke out between strikers and company guards at the auto parts manufacturer Perfect Circle. Eight were wounded and the governor called in the National Guard. Perfect Circle was the leading producer of piston rings in the country, hardly a small outfit. But it wasn't the Big Three, so the story of a small and courageous company standing up to the UAW took off in conservative circles. It figured prominently in the McClellan Committee hearings on union corruption in the Senate beginning in 1957. The hearings, of course, also made

Jimmy Hoffa a household name and dealt a blow to labor's public standing. The AFL-CIO expelled the Teamsters as a result, but considerable damage was already done. The favorability of unions in national polls fell over the committee's three-year existence.[27]

The questions about unions first batted around in the wake of New Deal legislation had come back in full force by the late 1950s. Unions appeared vulnerable. In the summer of 1958, the Republican Policy Committee in the Senate put out a handbook on "The Labor Bosses" packed with details from the McClellan Committee. GOP candidates for statewide office often "ran against" UAW head Walter Reuther rather than their actual opponent. The recession of 1958, dubbed the "Reuther recession" by conservative critics, was the worst in two decades and many saw unions to blame.[28]

Threatened by the recession and the first inklings of international competition, big companies pushed back. Across core industries, firms fought against cost-of-living adjustments and the power of stewards and union work rules in an attempt to gain more flexibility. Automakers floated the idea of an industry-wide lockout.[29] It was in this context that business leaders and many politicians rushed to put right-to-work on the ballot in several states, including heavily unionized ones. They had reason for optimism. When business leaders led a carefully orchestrated campaign for right-to-work in highly unionized Indiana the year before, unions were late to the game. They had no real answer to the critique of labor unions as bloated, outside special interests who were out to subvert the democratic process. This in a state where 40 percent of all workers belonged to unions!

The right-to-work campaigns of 1958 drew considerable resources from both sides. It was only against this rising storm that the national union movement began to take a more proactive role in state contests. Even into the mid-1950s, many unions still saw right-to-work as a southern phenomenon. The prospect of losing a second major Midwestern state forced the AFL-CIO to commit resources and expertise to the problem led by the IUD and Reuther. Nowhere was this more watched or contested than in the battle for the industrial heartland in Ohio. Labor's victory in Ohio was critical for unions in the region. Unions were successful in all but one state campaign (Kansas) that year, forcing the NRTWC to regroup. Right-to-work campaigns were scaled back in the aftermath. Some of the business interests behind the push began to question the usefulness of a state-by-state approach to target unions. More, the perceived overreach by business activists and politicians ended up costing Republicans dearly that year, especially in the Midwest. In Ohio, the unthinkable happened as John Bricker lost his Senate seat to the lightly regarded and perennial candidate Stephen Young.[30]

After labor's banner election and with a more receptive Congress coming in, most anticipated unions to ramp up their efforts to repeal Taft-Hartley. The consequences of the 1958 elections, however, were not straightforward. Unions first breathed a sigh of relief as most restrictive legislation in the states was tabled in the immediate aftermath. Right-to-work efforts in other industrialized states stalled. The business overreach also gave some life to long dormant progressive policies. In Wisconsin, activists had been quietly pushing for public-sector collective bargaining rights for years with little effect. New York City and Philadelphia recognized some public-sector unions at the end of the decade, but no statewide policies existed, even in the most highly unionized states. Efforts to enact state policies mostly stalled after Republican gains in 1946. Major public-sector unions like the American Federation of State, County and Municipal Workers (AFSCME) often had significant internal disagreement on whether to push for collective bargaining rights or to advocate through existing civil service laws. But in Wisconsin, the more favorable political climate and the weakened position of the most strident business activists provided the opening union activists and Democratic allies needed. Though only about a page long, the Wisconsin bill was strengthened in the coming years and provided a model for public-sector growth. The growth and ultimate success of public-sector unions was again highly uneven, including within the industrial Midwest.[31]

Labor did not find as warm of a reception in Congress. Unions still had to deal with the fallout from the McClellan Committee. Labor first tried to clean up its own house to ward off government restrictions. Expelling the Teamsters from the AFL-CIO and adopting a code of ethics were not enough to stop the Landrum-Griffin Act from becoming law in 1959. The act is the last major national labor law. It put checks on the power of union leaders by providing a bill of rights for union members that covered speech, the right to sue, and protections against disciplinary action by unions. It also required annual financial disclosures by unions to the Department of Labor, which were then available to employers and the public. Taft-Hartley repeal was not in the cards.[32]

At the bargaining table, big firms remained intransigent. U.S. Steel's chief negotiator Conrad Cooper took a hard line against union demands over work rules. The nationwide steel strike that summer was the biggest in history in terms of person-hours lost. The following year, GE stood out among large firms by keeping plants running during a strike and actively encouraging a back-to-work movement, delivering a major blow to the International Union of Electrical Workers (IUE) and its president, James Carey. At the dawn of the 1960s, industrial relations experts were asking if others would follow the GE strategy. It would take another decade as GE's more aggressive stance toward unions developed during the 1950s became common corporate practice by the late 1970s and 1980s.[33]

Business acceptance of unions and unions' ability to make a convincing case for labor rights were mixed at the peak of the capital–labor accord. There was wide variation across states, even within the industrial Midwest. This is not to suggest that the imagery of the capital–labor accord is all wrong. Gone were the days of union radicalism and the near revolutionary insurgency of the late 1930s and 1940s. The labor dynamo had indeed slowed down as Samuel Lubell described. Labor's broader ambitions for social justice, while always uneven, had dimmed considerably by the late 1950s. Yet employer resistance persisted. The hard-hitting questions about unions and the related policy proposals of the 1950s were crafted by sophisticated conservative organizations and were engaged by much larger audiences. Their critique of unions resonated with many. All this occurred at a time when unions were large, highly effective at the bargaining table, and when union gains often spilled over into the larger community.

Conclusion

This chapter presented an overview of labor relations in the 1950s, considering the space for labor influence and the considerable resistance to unionism in the business community. I have shown that while some parts of the capital–labor accord logic hold up well, such as the significant wage growth for average workers, it was clearly limited in geographic reach and in the willingness of firms to accept unions as legitimate bargaining partners and worker advocates. This peaked at the end of the decades as employers made a concerted push to curb unions in the industrial Midwest. I take this up in more detail in the next three chapters by examining campaigns over labor rights in Indiana, Ohio, and Wisconsin at the end of the 1950s.

3

Union Discord in Indiana

On Saturday March 2, 1957, more than ten thousand union members packed the statehouse grounds in Indianapolis. The scene was tense. The day before the Senate had approved a right-to-work bill and now it sat on Republican governor Harold Handley's desk. Indiana State Federation of Labor (ISFL) president Carl Mullen met privately with the governor, urging him to veto the bill while the legislature remained in session ready to respond. But after meeting with Mullen, the governor let the bill become law without his signature. He left through a back door to avoid the protesters. The *Indianapolis Star* described the whole affair as a blow to the prestige of union leaders, touting that "legislatures do not cringe when they crack the whip." When Mullen tried to explain the governor's position to the crowd, he was drowned out by boos.[1]

Indiana shocked the labor movement by becoming the first northern industrialized state to pass right-to-work. In this chapter, I analyze the campaigns waged by business and labor in order to understand how business succeeded in such a highly unionized state. Indiana leaned conservative, and that certainly helped the business cause, but the Republican-controlled legislature had made no real efforts to curb union organization in the decade leading up to the fight. I thus pay special attention to the key business and labor organizations involved and follow their efforts as they navigated institutional and grassroots arenas. Poor organization and an effective countermovement combined to sink labor in Indiana. Unions in Indiana, while certainly large and resourceful, were politically weak and disorganized at the height of the capital–labor accord. Labor's insider and outsider strategies appeared haphazard in comparison to the sophisticated business-led effort spearheaded by the Indiana Chamber of Commerce and the newly formed Indiana Right-to-Work Committee (INRTWC).

I begin by describing political opportunities and the state of labor and business organization in Indiana in the mid-twentieth century. I then provide a narrative account of the right-to-work campaign and show how the

Heartland Blues. Marc Dixon, Oxford University Press (2020). © Oxford University Press.
DOI: 10.1093/oso/9780190917036.001.0001.

outcome provided a jolt of confidence to business leaders and encouraged right-to-work activity elsewhere.

Indiana in the 1950s

By the 1950s, Indiana had a significant Republican lean in the state legislature and in general elections. Both parties were patronage based, precluding a strong role for unions in party politics. The lack of a citizen initiative option mostly confined fights over labor rights to the legislative process. All of this is to say that political opportunities for unions were somewhat limited. Labor's key advantage was its size. Unions were strong and effective at the bargaining table. Even here, however, organizational schisms and a lack of assistance from the national labor movement diminished labor's ability to mobilize its members and broader constituencies in the political process. These problems were not as pronounced in the business community.

Patronage Politics and the Conservative Tilt

Indiana was more of a "border state" than its Midwestern neighbors. The southern portion was settled first, shaped by migration from West Virginia and Kentucky. On the eve of the Civil War, Indiana's population had almost twice as many people from the South as did neighboring Ohio. The National Road, now Route 40, running east to west from Richmond to Terre Haute, historically divided the state. Those below it were more southern and traditional Democrats; those above it were more northern and Republican.[2]

The first half of the century saw the rise of giant industry. U.S. Steel "built" Gary, named after one of its founders, Elbert Henry Gary, in the far northwest of the state at the turn of the twentieth century, and other steelmakers soon followed. Like its neighbors in Illinois and Ohio, Indiana was a hotbed for Ku Klux Klan activity in the 1920s. By World War II, auto parts manufacturers dotted cities and towns across the northern half of the state from South Bend and Lafayette to Anderson and Kokomo. The UAW's second convention was held in South Bend. War industries also revived older industrial centers in the south like Evansville, while electronics manufacturing came to Bloomington. Over 40 percent of workers were in manufacturing by 1950. What remained, then, was a mix of mid-American conservative towns and

cities such as what Robert and Helen Lynd found in Muncie in their famous *Middletown* studies, giant industrial centers and company towns, particularly in the North, and traditional southern stretches below Route 40.
Outside of the new industrial centers, Republicans gained strength in most
places so that by the 1950s Indiana was marginally a two-party state with a
strong Republican lean in state elections. It went almost entirely Republican
in presidential races.[3]

Though the partisan lean did not bode well for labor, Indiana Republicans
had shown little interest in curbing labor. Party leaders instead focused on
selecting general election candidates amenable to an urbanizing and more
moderate state population, hard-right US Senator William Jenner notwithstanding. Whereas unions had achieved little in the way of progressive reform since World War II, Republican majority after Republican majority in
the legislature never expressed much interest in picking a fight. The party's
1956 platform stated that labor law should be changed only in consultation
with unions.[4]

Both parties were organized along patronage lines. The party who controlled the governor's office took 2 percent off the top of state employees' sal-
aries who were outside of the civil service, controlled license plate sales at
the county level, and actively sought donations from state vendors. Neither
party wanted to rock the boat as they each benefitted when in power. This arrangement was generally accepted by the public until the end of the decade
when a scandal erupted involving highway development and insider land
deals. In this context of patronage, party leaders saw no great need to court
unions. The industrial unions and the Indiana Industrial Union Council
(IUC) were one of many factions within the state Democratic Party, alongside city machines, liberals, and the traditional Democrats from rural areas
in the southern part of the state. Liberal and labor factions in the party were
typically too divided to wield much influence. Many union leaders from the
Building Trades identified as Republicans, and the ISFL was more likely to
work with Republicans, though it was less politically active overall.[5]

Business interests in the state worked through the Chamber of Commerce.
Because they did not take on party functions—for example, candidate selection, voter registration, and turnout—business organizations like
the Chamber posed no threat to the state party organizations, and their
relationships were less affected by the patronage structure than labor. A basic
"relationship of exchange" took hold. The Chamber of Commerce produced
a daily bulletin that was in high demand by legislators and held weekly

breakfasts during session at which they would honor a particular legislator for their service. Chamber leaders also dined and socialized at the same venues as legislators, including the exclusive Press and Columbia clubs in Indianapolis, which had no union staffers on their rolls.[6]

That business associations formed tight connections with legislators is hardly surprising. What is notable is the limited political operation by labor. Beyond party organization, unions tended not to participate in any of the pre-session study committees where support for various policies is often built. Melvin Kahn's study of Indiana labor politics found union lobbying tactics of the period to be crude. Whereas all but one of the Chamber lobbyists had a college degree, none of the union lobbyists did. Legislators often saw union lobbyists as boisterous and too "rah-rah." When the newly merged state AFL-CIO opened a hospitality room for legislators a few years after the right-to-work fight, its president Dallas Sells joked about the sparse attendance, noting that legislators were probably afraid to be seen with "labor goons."[7]

Union Organization

Union development in Indiana mirrored national trends and bore the imprint of the two major industries in the state in steel and auto. Violent steel strikes exploded and were repressed after World War I. After the labor movement bottomed out in the Depression, spurts of militancy—including a general strike in Terre Haute in 1935—led to organizing among the new CIO unions and the District 11 of the United Mine Workers. The war finally brought significant growth and stability. The state IUC formed in 1938 and claimed 64,000 members. At the end of the decade, steel making in the northwest of the state "had been cracked but not conquered by union organizers; the open shop was the rule in most Hoosier industrial centers; and company-dominated unions were common in many areas." Less than five years later, nearly all major industries were organized. Regional CIO director Powers Hapgood claimed in 1943 that the Indiana office staff no longer had time to go out and organize new shops as waves of workers were coming in on their own. Following the war, CIO union members outnumbered AFL members headed by giant UAW and USW locals. Thanks to the assistance of the National War Labor Board, the industrial unions in particular were able to stabilize their membership and negotiate union security clauses with employers.

By the mid-1950s, 40 percent of all workers belonged to unions and nearly 80 percent of union contracts had union security provisions. Steel and auto production alone accounted for nearly 14 percent of all workers in the state. The UAW and USW dominated the IUC. Industrial workers did quite well; the earnings of production workers in Indiana were in the 85th percentile nationally.[8]

While unions were highly successful at the bargaining table, they struggled with two problems the business community lacked. First, the labor movement in Indiana remained deeply divided long past the national merger of the AFL and CIO. Local leaders of the Building Trades unions resented the national CIO's allegiance to the Democratic Party. An Indiana Building Trades Council Leader put it this way in regard to the political vision of the CIO and UAW head Walter Reuther in particular: "Guys like Reuther attack the capitalist system and they're too blind to recognize that if business doesn't prosper then labor won't do worth a damn." According to state CIO leaders, the Building Trades saw COPE (and the CIO PAC before it) as a "bad word" not to be used. In their merger talks, an ISFL leader allegedly grilled Lester Thornton from the steelworkers on the point of a political education program, asking "[E]ducation? What are we going to educate these people for?" Such differences in politics and outlook were not unique to Indiana, but they were more pronounced here and lingered longer than most. Some Building Trades unions whose parent organizations joined the national AFL-CIO in the 1955 merger steadfastly refused to do so in Indiana for the next decade.[9]

Despite their differences, the two bodies developed a unified political platform at a meeting in March 1956, and they agreed to share space in the next legislative session. A joint committee of ISFL and IUC unions presented it to both Republican and Democratic platform committees. This gave the IUC hope for a quick merger. But discussions slowed as the ISFL insisted that Carl Mullen be the president of the merged federation even though the ISFL had fewer members. The final split came in the governor's race. The IUC endorsed long-shot Democratic candidate and Terre Haute mayor Ralph Tucker over World War II veteran and Republican lieutenant governor Harold Handley. The ISFL remained neutral because Handley had refused to endorse right-to-work on the campaign trail. Handley ended up coasting to an easy victory on the national wave of support for Eisenhower while Republicans made large gains in the statehouse, holding commanding 33–17 and 75–24 majorities in the Senate and House, respectively. Following the election, Mullen informed his CIO counterpart Dallas Sells that the merger committee had been replaced by the ISFL executive board and all discussions would cease until after the legislative session. The IUC and the ISFL then scrapped their plans to share space and coordinate during the 1957 legislative session.[10]

Union divisions went beyond traditional craft–industrial divides. The UAW and the Steelworkers, and their respective regional directors in Ray Berndt and Jim Robb, were often at odds as they sought control of the IUC, for which UAW officer Dallas Sells served as president. Even within the Steelworkers, spats between the northern district and its smaller counterpart in the southern part of the state sometimes required the intervention of international union president David McDonald. There were splits in the business community, too, of course. The giant manufacturers in the state—Big Steel and Big Auto—were typically hesitant to touch any controversial issue, unlike many smaller manufacturers. Yet, unlike labor, almost all business political action worked through the state chamber and most fissures remained in-house. The new political organization on the scene, the INRTWC, worked through the chamber as well.

The second problem for the Indiana labor moment was that local unionists and the two state federations were left on their own in important ways. They received little assistance or input from the national labor movement. Even at the peak of postwar union strength, and at a moment when union staffs were expanding in size and sophistication, state politics was often an afterthought for labor. This varied within the region. As we will see, the labor movement in neighboring Michigan had a highly active political program with the support of the UAW. Indeed, large international unions like the USW and especially the UAW had sophisticated political programs, not to mention the national AFL-CIO's COPE. Most labor personnel and expertise were directed toward Washington, DC; they turned to the states for big elections or to trouble-shoot crises. This is in contrast to business peak associations like the NAM and the Chamber, both of whom poured significant resources into state politics on the labor front, often in union strongholds. As of 1956, the NAM was working with state affiliates across the Midwest to forge right-to-work groups and campaigns. In early 1957, US Chamber of Commerce president John Coleman toured several large and highly unionized cities to engage local leaders on the topic.[11]

This brief sketch shows a divided labor movement without many political allies. To this point, however, there had been no concerted push for restrictions on labor unions. The Chamber needed to shake legislators out of their routines and to push a mostly nonideological party leadership to take on a controversial issue and a tough stance on labor.

The Right-to-Work Campaign

Rumblings for right-to-work grew out of an explosive labor conflict at the Perfect Circle auto parts plant in New Castle, fifty miles east of Indianapolis. Industrial unions had secured big gains in their negotiations with large ol-igopolistic firms since the war. Smaller, often family-owned manufacturers were much less inclined to go along for both financial and ideological reasons. Perfect Circle, while the largest volume producer of piston rings in the country, was clearly in the latter group. The UAW gained a foothold at the company during World War II with the assistance of the National War Labor Board, but union gains were uneven in the following years. When the union struck for a single wage within the auto parts sector in 1948, the company kept the plants running, provided bonuses to nonstrikers, and outlasted the union. In 1955, the company again took a hard line in their negotiations with the UAW and took special issue with the UAW's demand for the union shop. When a strike ensued and the company again kept its plants running, scuffles and vandalism predictably broke out. But on October 5, things took a much darker turn. A crowd of two thousand strikers and union supporters gathered outside the foundry's gates to protest the sacking of some strikers when a company guard fired into the crowd. Several strikers rushed home to get their guns, and shooting broke out on both sides, wounding eight. Republican governor George Craig called in the National Guard and estab-lished marshal law, effectively crippling the strike.[12]

Perfect Circle vice president William Prosser drew cheers from manage-ment circles for standing up for the individual's right to work against "com-pulsory unionism." Along with Herb Kohler in Wisconsin, Prosser became one of the leading faces of business resistance to the labor movement. "The union has a perfect right to strike," Prosser told the *Wall Street Journal*. "We keep the factories open believing that those who want to work also have a perfect right to work." As historian David Anderson describes, the story of a courageous company in the heartland standing up to Big Labor, and protecting the right to work no less, became a cause célèbre in conservative circles. The Perfect Circle story was featured in the McClellan Committee hearings in the US Senate in 1958, where Prosser blamed UAW officials for

the violent conflict. Closer to home, New Castle resident and future lieutenant governor Crawford Parker became one of the most vocal advocates of
right-to-work in the state. The immediate outcome was a significant blow to
the UAW. The union was ousted in decertification elections at Perfect Circle
plants in nearby Richmond and Hagerstown, and it was forced to agree to
company terms in New Castle.[13]

That same year the NRTWC opened their doors to assist and grow state
campaigns around the country. Indianapolis businessmen had already
begun meeting about a potential campaign. The press coverage of the strike
alone provided a ready-made rationale: unions were big, sometimes violent and out of control, and trampled on the rights of individual employees
and employers. Governor Craig, speaking during the dispute, put it this
way: "[T]he right of local self determination apparently has been usurped by
professional bureaucracy in Detroit." This local flavor alongside the by then
ubiquitous right-to-work materials churned out by the NAM and to a lesser
extent the NRTWC helped shape business's public case for right-to-work.
By 1955, the NAM had honed in on the "bigness" of labor and the power of
union leaders as a pressing threat to freedom.[14]

The Indianapolis Chamber of Commerce organized meetings with local
employers in 1955 and formed the INRTWC in February 1956, headed by
publisher Stephen Noland. Noland graduated from Harvard in 1914 and was
a lieutenant in an artillery regiment during World War I before spending
most of his career as a journalist. As a young man, he had interviewed Samuel
Gompers and liked to paraphrase the late AFL leader when making a case
for right-to-work. As chair of the INRTWC, he sought out disaffected union
members and aggrieved employers like Perfect Circle to be the face of the
issue. A longtime supporter of Republican causes, Noland took on a more
public role after touring Britain in 1949. Upon return, he wrote a series of
commentaries on "Life under Socialism in Britain" and gave talks across the
state on the dangers of Labor Party rule.[15]

It is not clear how many union members the INRTWC actually recruited.
There are no state membership records. A Group Research report found
75 percent of the national parent organization's members to be businesses.
Still, the workers the INRTWC did recruit were visible. Disgruntled former
unionist and railroad engineer Lafayette Hooser served as its vice president
and was often sought out by reporters. Throughout 1956, Noland and Hooser
hit the speaking circuit touting right-to-work at local Kiwanians Clubs,
Chambers of Commerce, and other community organizations.[16]

The INRTWC drew on the organizational resources and expertise of the Indiana Chamber of Commerce and its executive director, Jack Reich (some unionists labeled the effort "Reich-to-Work"). Other partners included the Associated Employers of Indiana, the Indiana Manufacturers Association, and mid-sized manufacturers like International Steel and the Indiana Brass Company. Some of the largest corporations with a presence in the state, such as big steel makers and automakers, did not take a public stand on the issue, while J. Irwin Miller, the CEO of Columbus-based engine manufacturer Cummings, publicly opposed right-to-work.[17] Because of the ambivalence among larger firms, right-to-work was often seen as a small business crusade. This face of right-to-work as small-business-led and sometimes reactionary—the followers of former Notre Dame dean Clarence Manion and his popular radio forum—rings true to a degree. Perhaps more accurate, however, is that right-to-work was a multipronged effort.[18] The most prominent brand-name manufacturers mostly stayed out of the campaigns nationally (with some notable exceptions of General Electric and Boeing). But they contributed to trade and political associations that did promote right-to-work. Moreover, several large *Fortune 500* manufacturers participated in right-to-work efforts, as witnessed in Ohio. The Indiana campaign minimized any public splits by directing all action through the Chamber of Commerce.

The business campaign had done significant outreach by the beginning of the 1957 legislative session. An early February poll conducted for the Pulliam-owned *Indianapolis News* found majority support for right-to-work but that a large share of respondents still did not know what it was. To demonstrate public support and awareness, the Chamber borrowed the Working Together program model from their national organization whereby local chamber groups sponsored discussions on right-to-work and invited other civic groups to participate. They provided individuals with personalized scripts to use when calling on elected officials. More than 2,500 business owners and managers participated. Individual contributions ranged from talking to legislators, to mundane tasks like helping with mailings or talking with neighbors, to engaging other civic groups on the issue. The INRTWC also went beyond their business base and sought out dissident union members to testify on the issue, and they persuaded incoming lieutenant governor Crawford Parker and George Hinkle, a former union official and commissioner of labor in the Craig administration, to publicly endorse right-to-work.[19]

The ISFL executive board met in December of 1956 to strategize on right-to-work and the upcoming session. Their basic plan hinged on Republican governor Harold Handley. They refused to endorse his Democratic opponent in the governor's race partly because they believed that Handley would veto right-to-work if it came to that. Governor Handley reinforced this view at the beginning of the legislative session when he stated that he preferred a minimum of government interference in labor–management relations. The IUC was not much more active. IUC members discussed right-to-work at their March convention in 1956, and at least one UAW local began mailing information to their members prior to the fall elections. However, it was not until right-to-work bills were introduced in the House and Senate that labor activity picked up.

The labor campaign was mostly an insular affair. In January and February, local unions and central labor councils held meetings with union members on the issue. Lobbyists from the larger unions and from both state federations met with legislators. Republican unionists from the Building Trades also met state GOP leadership. In short, unions followed a familiar path of lobbying and testifying at public hearings. The ISFL executive board summed up their strategy in retrospect: "We still believed that though we had elected conservative legislators, by organizing our forces in a solid front and with the support of our loyal friends, we could stop this bad legislation."[20]

After there was some momentum behind the right-to-work bills, international union presidents and AFL-CIO president George Meany flooded legislators with telegrams and mass mailings. United Brotherhood of Carpenters' president Maurice Hutchinson sent a telegram to all GOP legislators as a prominent Labor Republican. These efforts mostly missed the mark. The Republican Caucus Chairman in the House claimed that less than a quarter of the postcards he received were actually signed by people in his district. A survey of legislators two years later found that most disregarded the mass labor mailings altogether.[21]

The House and Senate public hearings on their respective right-to-work bills in early February 1957 provide an instructive contrast of the two campaigns. Unions packed both hearings with supporters. At the Senate hearing, IUC president Dallas Sells gave a carefully prepared speech associating right-to-work with the enemies of the union movement. But things took an embarrassing turn for labor when Cecil Roeder, from Sells's own local union at the Delco-Remy plant in Anderson, proudly wore his UAW cap as he testified *in favor* of the bill. Sells had grown up in Anderson. He started as an industrial electrician at the giant Delco-Remy plant in the late 1930s and became president of the UAW local in 1951 before heading the IUC. At the hearing, Roeder testified that right-to-work will "give the union back to its membership."

All the INRTWC presentations stayed on point casting right-to-work as a necessary protection for the individual employee against unresponsive unions and the abuses of labor leaders. Mary Crabtree, an IBEW member at RCA, stated she supported right-to-work because she didn't agree with the unions' political views but had no way out: "I have been a member for nine years, and have not yet found any effective way to protest any policy." The one employer represented was Perfect Circle. Vice president William Prosser invoked the riotous scene of the New Castle strike before the packed audience. "A minority of our workers tried to force their will on the majority," he told the committee, noting also how the UAW warned him it would be a violent strike.

After the hearings the *Indianapolis Star* printed a cartoon pitting an earnest, older legislator against an ape-like, cigar-chomping union boss on right-to-work, asking "Who's Boss Around Here?" The disparaging caricature tapped into a critical problem for the union campaign (see Figure 3.1). Proponents in the legislature convincingly argued that it was not union members who were against right-to-work, just union leaders. Indeed, the only union members testifying did so on behalf of the INRTWC.[22]

These stumbles notwithstanding, and even with large Republican majorities in both chambers, many legislators were still wary of touching the hot-button issue. Halfway through the legislative session, neither the House nor the Senate had moved their respective right-to-work bills out of committee, and most thought the issue would die there. Serious political will was needed to pass right-to-work in a state with 40 percent union density. Governor Handley offered no public support for right-to-work nor did he push fellow Republicans behind the scenes; House majority leader Robert Webb from heavily unionized Lake County was opposed to the measure.[23] What right-to-work backers needed was a strong push by an ambitious politician or two who would link their career to its advancement. They found two in House speaker George Diener from Indianapolis and especially lieutenant governor Crawford Parker. Both had higher aspirations. Diener had risen to speaker after just two terms in the legislature, while Parker had worked his way up from local party activist and county chair to secretary of state and to lieutenant governor. In staking out a forceful position on right-to-work, Parker

Figure 3.1 Unions versus the Legislature in the Right-to-Work Debate

The cartoon appeared in *The Indianapolis Star* on Friday, February 8, 1957, p. 16. Courtesy of PARS International Corp.

was able to distinguish himself from the governor and other leaders in the legislature to good effect. He received the party's gubernatorial nomination in 1960.[24]

Right-to-work advocates also found some luck. With both bills fizzling in committee, violence flared in a Machinists' strike in Princeton in the southwest corner of the state. On February 12, someone shot into the home of a nonstriker in neighboring Oakland City and wounded a four-month-old baby. Governor Handley ordered state troopers in to hunt down the shooter in what looked to be another ugly labor incident. Right-to-work advocates moved quickly; the episode immediately figured into campaign materials portraying unions as violent and out of control. Edward Greenfield, the local minister who led the "back-to-work" movement in Princeton, was put under police protection after receiving threats. He told his story in a NRTWC pamphlet *The Anatomy of a Wildcat*. The NRTWC even made a film inspired by the events titled *And Women Must Weep!*[25]

The shooting undoubtedly gave some legs to the House bill. Company president Richard Brumfield provided legislators with talking points when describing the event in terms of union coercion and the right-to-work, calling it "a new low in the use of violence as a threat against employees who have a right to work." The House bill's cosponsor Arthur Atwell pointed to the violence in the Princeton strike as more evidence of the need for union restrictions and the House Labor Committee voted the bill to the floor within days of the incident. A week later the Republican-dominated House passed right-to-work by twelve votes.[26]

There was still no movement in the Senate where the Labor Committee chairman Roy Conrad, a Republican from Monticello, sat on the bill. Here Parker singlehandedly gave it life. On Monday, February 25, Parker opened Senate proceedings with the unprecedented move of assigning right-to-work to the Senate Committee of the Whole. This amounted to asking the entire body to vote it out of committee to themselves. Senate minority leader Matthew Welsh of Vincennes protested because the body did not have the bill in front of them but was ruled out of order. A motion by Welsh to recommit the bill to the Labor Committee carried by two votes, but two senators switched before the Senate reconvened. This created a tie, which Parker then broke. After more than four hours of parliamentary wrangling, right-to-work backers scored the decisive victory by voting it out of the Committee of the Whole to the Senate body by two votes. After the unorthodox move by Parker, additional Republicans agreed to back the measure. All union supporters could do at this point was try to cripple the bill with amendments. Right-to-work passed the Senate by a narrow four-vote margin on Friday, March 1, and Governor Handley let it become law without his signature.[27]

The last-minute surprise of labor violence in Oakland City and the unprecedented maneuvering by Parker caught unions off guard. These contingencies, however, mask some of the more general problems labor faced. Unions lacked good working relationships in the legislature and could not persuade many beyond their closest supporters. Considering roll call votes from that session, thirty-five out of forty Democrats across both chambers voted against right-to-work, though they could not prevent a Democrat from cosponsoring right-to-work in the House. The 90th General Assembly included six union members. Eleven more had at least some prior union affiliation. Of these seventeen potentially union-friendly legislators, none voted for right-to-work. Considering a broader range of ten other pertinent labor policies up for a vote, including changes in unemployment insurance and workers compensation, all of these legislators with at least some union experience voted with labor on a majority of the bills. But unions had no success in reaching legislators beyond these friendly confines. Seventy percent of Republicans voted for right-to-work. This percentage does not change for those from heavily industrialized districts. While Republicans held commanding majorities in both chambers, they had held large majorities for the last *seventeen years* and had not brought right-to-work to a vote. Party leaders, at least, had expressed little interest in the issue. The Chamber and the INRTWC campaign pushed them to move on a controversial issue most were hesitant to touch. Once they did, unions could not stop them.[28]

Union (Dis)organization and the Right-to-Work Outcome

More than anything else, poor union organization and an effective countermovement doomed labor in the right-to-work fight. Political opportunities were admittedly limited for labor unions in Indiana. Employers, by contrast, benefited from favorable relationships with legislators. However, this alone was not enough to push legislators to embrace a controversial labor issue in a heavily unionized state. Stark organizational differences between business and labor shaped the range and effectiveness of insider and outsider strategies adopted by each side and the ability of unions to keep up with the pace of the business campaign. Union infighting and the lack of professional assistance and expertise from the national labor movement limited union member participation, framing, and outreach on right-to-work, all in stark comparison to the Chamber and INRTWC. This made an already limited opportunity context much worse.

Two events at the end of the legislative fight begin to capture labor's organizational deficits when it comes to infighting. First, after it became clear that the Senate was going to pass the bill, Building Trades leaders sought to cut their own deal. Their supporters in the legislature introduced a last-minute amendment to exempt most craft unions from the bill. The motion to amend failed by only two votes, but the IUC was furious.[29] Second, despite the last-minute overtures from the Building Trades, right-to-work passed the Senate on Friday, March 1. The next day the ISFL led a demonstration at the statehouse to pressure Governor Handley to veto the bill. The ISFL claimed 25,000 protesters while media reports were closer to 10,000. Clear from both accounts, the industrial unions of the IUC boycotted the event entirely. The only protest during the right-to-work campaign was marked as much by union divisions as it was a show of strength.[30]

Intramovement conflict became dysfunctional in Indiana. The spat between the ISFL and IUC—sometimes public, sometimes under the radar—was laid bare in the aftermath of the vote. Otto Suhr of the Carpenters union protested that the IUC and UAW in particular did nothing to stop right-to-work: "I believe that they did not want [ISFL president] Carl Mullen to get the credit for stopping the bill." The ISFL executive board went further. In a letter to AFL-CIO president George Meany, the board claimed that the IUC sunk the effort:

> During the meeting of the General Assembly, the officers of the State Industrial Union Council did not join with us, as they previously promised . . . but held aloof in more or less criticism of our efforts to stop the Right-to-Work Bill. Bad press statements were made which placed us on the defensive and encouraged the anti-labor forces . . . it is our conviction that orders were being given through the regional organizations of the two large unions—Steel and Auto.[31]

The attack on the IUC as being aloof during the conflict holds some truth. While they clearly fought against right-to-work, IUC leaders questioned the usefulness of dropping everything else for the fight as the ISFL had done. Instead, they pursued the general political program both bodies agreed to in 1956. District 31 head for the steelworkers Lester Thornton's account of the effort amounted to an "I told you so" critique of the ISFL and their big bet on Governor Handley:

> Maybe he [Mullen] thought he was under the gun on that one, since had introduced Handley to his convention and supported his candidacy and since there was no indication that Handley was going to veto the bill if passed. Maybe he thought he was under the gun and better concentrated all his efforts on that legislation and forget everything else.[32]

A postmortem of the campaign by the labor-based Indiana Council for Industrial Peace (it formed after the 1957 fight) reached a similar conclusion on infighting and the lack of coordination, though it did not take sides in the ISFL-IUC spat. What is clear is that the persistent schisms limited even the most basic attempts to produce a united front against right-to-work and made the pro-right-to-work effort appear seamless in contrast. It was not, of course. The giant manufacturers never backed right-to-work publicly. Yet the business campaign successfully muted most opposition. All of the local Chamber of Commerce affiliates got behind the issue as did the other trade associations in the state. The INRTWC worked as an offshoot of the Chamber.

Union schisms were not the only organizational problem. The national labor movement—the AFL-CIO and the large international unions—offered little in the way of staff or expertise to counter the business campaign. Within labor circles, right-to-work was typically seen as a problem relegated to the South, a region many unions had given up on organizing. The involvement of the national labor movement in right-to-work for most of the 1950s was limited to a series of flyers and talking points produced by the research departments of the rival federations. The CIO published *The Case against "Right to Work" Laws* in 1954. The AFL's newspaper *The American Federationist* ran a series of articles on right-to-work in 1955. A NAM survey of these union talking points identified labor's key arguments as mostly defensive: right-to-work does not guarantee anyone a job and is hypocritical; union security is a fundamental means of self-protection for labor; union security is about majority rule, like other Democratic arrangements; and union security prevents free-riders. Public testimony and statements to the press by union leaders in Indiana did not stray too far from this basic script, though they tended to be cruder. Noting the hypocrisy of right-to-work backers, Peter Terzick of the Carpenters told the Senate Labor Committee that the "bleeding hearts for the poor workers [the INRTWC] could better spend their time helping the people of Indiana to get more than 50 cents an hour."[33]

There was a new labor development on right-to-work that the NAM actually feared. This was the "morality angle" and the increasingly critical stance of religious leaders toward right-to-work. Elizabeth Fones-Wolf's research shows how labor, and the CIO in particular, had worked to cultivate religious ties for more than a decade before right-to-work took off in the Midwest, beginning with the appointment of steelworker and evangelical Protestant John Ramsay as their religious liaison. On right-to-work, the steelworkers helped Father Jerome Turner publish a critical assessment in *The Closed Shop*. The NAM was worried enough to recruit their own religious authority in Father Edward A. Keller of Notre Dame. Notably, little of this made its way into the disorganized labor campaign, nor did the AFL-CIO offer help. Aside from distributing literature to international unions and state affiliates, there was no attempt by the AFL-CIO to help forge actual campaigns. One Presbyterian minister from Indianapolis spoke against right-to-work, but there was no coordinated attempt to mobilize clergy on labor's behalf or to forge a broader labor–faith coalition. Staff from international unions were similarly distant. National steelworker officials did not come to Indianapolis until the Senate bill was on the verge of passage, while other national union participation amounted to a stream of telegrams to legislators at the end.[34]

Unions in Indiana had enough difficulty forging a united labor front, so it is not entirely surprising they did not seek other coalition partners. The marked divisions within the labor movement notwithstanding, many union activists had a hard time envisioning a broader coalition involving clergy and labor's place in it. Early in the session, the Senate briefly discussed putting right-to-work on the ballot as a legislative referendum. It did not gain any traction, but ISFL president Carl Mullen's opinion is instructive. He argued that a public referendum was unfair because it would allow everyone to vote on a matter only affecting the working class. This view of the labor movement, while not unusual for someone in Mullen's position, precluded any larger public stake in labor rights. The IUC and its bigger member unions in the state likewise did not look beyond the boundaries of the labor movement to make their case. Worse for Indiana unions, the public face of the labor campaign was limited to union leaders. Rank-and-file union members were mostly in the background, save for a last-ditch protest. The only union members testifying were those brought in by the INRWTC in *support* of right-to-work. It is not surprising that in this context the claims made by unions were almost entirely defensive in nature.

A broader coalition of labor and faith may not have worked once right-to-work gained momentum. Still, it is clear that business feared this possibility. It is also clear that, in its absence, the insular and divided labor campaign with union leaders as its public face made unions vulnerable to key business claims. The Chamber of Commerce mostly lacked the organizational deficits of labor. In addition to routine access to legislators, it had two things going for it. First, it was well-organized from the top. The Chamber's executive vice president and chief lobbyist Jack Reich was highly regarded by legislators and opponents alike. Dissenting opinions within the business community were effectively minimized. Second, it reached beyond its base to convey a larger stake in the issue than the self-interest of employers. Following the lead of its parent organization, the INRTWC recruited union members. INRTWC head Stephen Noland credited union members as his most powerful ammunition for right-to-work. This allowed the business campaign to more credibly claim that right-to-work was needed to protect *employees* from union abuses.

An alternative interpretation is that political opportunities precluded a contest altogether and that these organizational and strategic differences between business and labor were secondary. Here, Indiana, as more of a border state, was more conservative than its Midwestern neighbors and thus more inclined to pass right-to-work from the start. Large Republican majorities in both houses clearly made the legislation possible. Yet while conservatism helped, it does not stand on its own as an explanation for two reasons. First, public understanding of the issue was limited. Among those who understood the issue better—union members—there was considerable support for union security clauses. The union shop authorization polls conducted by the NLRB for three years after the passage of the Taft-Hartley Act show 90 percent of Indiana workers in unionized establishments voting in favor of union security. Second, and in the absence of any public groundswell, conservative, Republican-controlled legislatures in the decade and a half leading up to the fight had never pushed right-to-work. As Dallas Sells recalled, right-to-work just was not an issue before in the region. Instead, organization, and the comparatively sophisticated mobilization by the Chamber, was critical in pushing the legislature to take on a controversial issue with a clear and sizeable opposition and then steering it through.[35]

The Aftermath

Labor supporters did manage a minor victory in the right-to-work battle. They were able to strike an emergency clause from the bill. This delayed the implementation of the law and allowed time for some unions to negotiate new and lengthy contracts, pushing the onset of right-to-work back further. The immediate consequence of the passage of right-to-work for the Indiana labor movement was a hastening of the merger negotiations between the ISFL and the IUC. This came from the top. AFL-CIO president George Meany pushed the rival federations to merge in the fall of 1957. IUC president Dallas Sells became the head of the merged state AFL-CIO.

Labor made a more concerted and coordinated organized attempt to re- peal right-to-work in the coming years. Even here, however, efforts were slow to get off the ground because of intramovement dissension, this time disagreements between the steelworkers and the UAW, and by extension state AFL-CIO leader Dallas Sells. The repeal effort was accompanied by legal challenges that slowly whittled away at right-to-work. The authors of the bill somehow did not explicitly forbid the agency shop (requiring fees for service but not requiring actual union membership). After GM refused to bargain with the UAW on the issue of the agency shop in Indiana, the union appealed to the NLRB. The board initially decided against the UAW. However, the union tried again with a more labor-friendly composition ap- pointed by President Kennedy and the NRLB reversed the earlier decision. In the legislature, unions were successful in getting the state Democratic Party behind repeal efforts by the early 1960s. In 1964, Democratic gubernato- rial candidate Roger Branigan stated he would repeal the bill if elected. And unions benefitted from the nationwide liberal, anti-Goldwater wave that year as Democrats won majorities in both the House and Senate for the first time since 1936 and Branigan won the governor's race. The repeal bill was given high priority and passed in March of 1965. The fanfare was muted in com- parison to the 1957 fight.[36]

The right-to-work fallout had a second and more far-reaching effect: right- to-work immediately became a national issue after Indiana. The AFL-CIO was forced to take more of an interest in state fights. The business success in heavily unionized Indiana coupled with revelations of union corruption from the McClellan Committee provided many business leaders with an extra jolt of confidence in their dealings with labor. Right-to-work measures were placed on the ballot in several states in 1958. Nowhere was this more hotly contested than in neighboring Ohio, a campaign I turn to in the next chapter.

Conclusion

For all the fears stoked about Big Labor, unions were politically weak and dis- organized in Indiana. With a well-organized opposition and a cool reception from the legislature, unions in Indiana needed to make a more assertive case in the right-to-work fight. This chapter has shown how deep divisions com- plicated everything for the labor campaign, from lobbying, to mobilizing union members, to forging broader coalitions and staging protests. What is more, local unions and the rival state federations were left on their own to counter right-to-work. While union political programs were growing in size and sophistication, state politics was not on the radar. There was a gap between the skills and expertise in Washington, DC, and the organizations charged to carry out the right-to-work fight in Indiana. These organizational deficits made an already limited opportunity context much worse for labor.

Just as important as labor's follies was a well-organized countermovement headed by the Chamber of Commerce. In the right-to-work campaign, business had routine access to legislators. It was not shut out by patronage party organizations in the same way as labor. Yet, even with these favorable circumstances, the Chamber and affiliated organizations still did the work to push legislators to take on a controversial issue. Local business leaders gave the Chamber's campaign legitimacy by holding meetings on the issue in their communities, contacting their representatives directly, reaching beyond their constituency, and recruiting union members. Unions did not match this outreach or secure the support of allies outside of the labor movement.

Indiana was a breakthrough for business activism in the states. Interviewed during the post–World War II strike wave, Indianapolis Chamber of Commerce executive William Book was among the many business leaders worried about an insurgent labor movement and the direction of the country: "I believe there are people who would like to see an end of the profit system. The strikes are just an effervescence of the underlying causes." Twelve years later he could bask in the right-to-work victory and the hard work business organizations had done to spread the "gospel of conservatism" in the Hoosier state. "While Indiana is traditionally a conservative, independent state," he told *Nation's Business* in 1957, "it didn't just happen that way."[37] The change of fortunes for William Book and the Indiana business community mirrors national developments in many ways. Union moderation in the early postwar years was accompanied by increasing resistance and organizing by the business community. But Indiana stood out. Forty percent of all workers belonged to unions. The right-to-work effort was not easy or neat; the practical politics on the ground indeed required some extraordinary measures. The lieutenant governor broke parliamentary ground in treating the Senate as the Committee of the Whole to give the bill life. In the end, the national Chamber of Commerce could tout the Indiana model as a way to curb unions.

4

Flipping the Script in Ohio

On July 21, 1958, a group of about thirty business leaders and political operatives met at the exclusive Queen City Club in Cincinnati. At issue was whether to go through with putting right-to-work on the ballot that fall. The Ohio Chamber of Commerce launched the right-to-work campaign the year before, and signatures to put the measure on the ballot were due to the secretary of state's office in a couple of weeks. Republican leaders objected that the controversial labor issue could damage the entire ticket. US Senator John Bricker pleaded with the group to put the issue off for another year. But the business leaders in the room, including representatives from General Electric and Proctor and Gamble among others, scoffed at the idea of tabling right-to-work. They were convinced that the time to curb unions was now. Bricker left the meeting seething. Two days later, the Chamber's front group, Ohioans for Right-to-Work (OHRTW), delivered the necessary signatures to the Secretary of State's office.[1]

Emboldened by the victory in highly unionized Indiana in 1957 and the sensational allegations of union corruption emerging from the McClellan Committee in 1958, business leaders pushed ahead even when their more cautious political allies warned against it. After Indiana, right-to-work became a national issue. Six states put right-to-work on the ballot the following year. Right-to-work organizations formed across the Midwest; the NRTWC began taking out ads in Michigan newspapers. And the Ohio campaign was the center of it all. The surprisingly lopsided defeat of right-to-work there slowed its momentum in the industrial Midwest and opened the door to more progressive action on labor policy.

This chapter analyzes the campaigns waged by business and labor in the buckeye state. I show why business leaders had good reason to be confident at the outset and then how unions effectively flipped the script from Indiana. Labor succeeded in Ohio due to solid organization and an unusually broad coalition, a development aided by the more active role of the national labor movement in the conflict. The coalition allowed unions to move away from a purely defensive approach to right-to-work and to keep union leaders from

Heartland Blues. Marc Dixon, Oxford University Press (2020). © Oxford University Press.
DOI: 10.1093/oso/9780190917036.001.0001.

becoming the focus as they had in prior campaigns. By contrast, the Ohio Chamber of Commerce and OHRTW struggled to mobilize some of their closest allies. Notable in this case is that neither party establishment wanted to touch right-to-work.

Like the previous chapter, I begin by describing political opportunities and the state of labor and business organization, including the more wide-open forum of the ballot initiative. I then provide a narrative account of the right-to-work campaign and consider the implications of its defeat for labor rights in the Midwest and beyond.

Ohio in the 1950s

Ohio was a conservative-leaning state headed by a strong Republican Party organized out of Cincinnati and marked by general dysfunction on the left. Early settlement patterns and the industrial chaos of the 1930s combined to produce a relatively stable political geography that shifted along a diagonal from conservative strength in the southwest of the state to liberal pockets in the northeast. Large portions of the state were settled by Whigs from New England and Kentucky, producing predictably Republican counties that stretched across central and southwestern Ohio. Corn Belt farmers across the western half of the state—more prosperous than farmers elsewhere—likewise proved a reliable Republican base.

Large-scale steel, auto, and rubber production came to dominate the northeastern corner of the state in the early twentieth century. This region was hit harder by the Great Depression than elsewhere, and the industrial conflict there was much bloodier. The unrest of the 1930s was punctuated by the Little Steel strike of 1937. Whereas US Steel surprisingly reached a quick agreement with the Steel Workers Organizing Committee (SWOC), many of its smaller, though still large, counterparts refused to budge. When SWOC struck that spring, Republic, Youngstown Sheet and Tube, Inland, and Bethlehem Steel dug in. They armed themselves and kept their plants running. Riots and violent conflicts ensued across the region. Six strikers were killed in Ohio and scores more injured. Core union supporters on the picket lines from Cleveland to Canton and Youngstown were often foreign-born. Here families were more likely to welcome the New Deal state and basic labor rights as a solution to their problems. While northeast Ohio and other industrial and mining centers in the state went Democratic during the turbulent 1930s, most of rural Ohio remained wary of government and unions.[2]

Political Dysfunction on the Left

Industrial development and the labor insurgency of the 1930s produced a sizeable demographic seemingly open to labor and liberal claims. Still, no organizations had proven capable of translating this into any progressive, working-class politics during the 1950s. In 1958, Democratic pollster Louis Harris and Associates concluded that Ohio Democrats were "a sleeping giant that neither any candidate nor organization leader has aroused" since World War II. "In a state in which the industrial worker population and organized labor total runs among the leaders, it is almost incredible to report . . . [that] one of the leading right-wing Republicans in the country[,] John W. Bricker, has amassed close to 50 percent of the trade union vote."[3]

Democrats and unions were both disorganized. Democratic Party organization was fiercely local and amounted to a series of fiefdoms across the large and mid-sized industrial cities of the state. Political scientist John Fenton concluded that "[T]here was, in fact, no statewide Democratic Party in Ohio. The state's Democratic Party was an aggregation of city machines which had little or no interest in statewide elections unless the candidate was from their city." Unions, no matter how big, had no reliable place in this decentralized arrangement, nor in the more organized Republican Party, and had little sway in state government as a result. The UAW and the Steelworkers were the two largest unions in Ohio as in Indiana. But there were scores of unions, small and large, with no one dominant. Individual union leaders often cut their own deals with candidates and most, whether industrial or craft, eschewed larger social objectives beyond the wages and working conditions of their members.[4]

The 1950 election for US Senate in Ohio is Exhibit A of Democratic Party and union dysfunction. Robert Taft faced the electorate for the first time since the passage of the anti-labor Taft-Hartley Act of 1947. State auditor Joseph Ferguson emerged out of a lackluster field of seven Democratic candidates to face Taft, though some Democrats, including conservative governor Frank Lausche, refused to endorse him. The CIO-PAC made defeating Taft its number-one priority for the congressional election cycle. The PAC's national director Jack Kroll lived in Cincinnati and assured that resources would not be a problem. The CIO deployed 800 Election Day workers to Cleveland, more than anywhere else in the country. AFL president and former Ohio state senator William Green likewise stepped up resources. Ohio AFL and CIO unions even formed a short-lived United Labor Committee. With the state's business community equally resolute behind Taft, the *New York Times* described the contest as having the feel of a "class struggle" with the fate of the New Deal at stake. It turned out to be a rout. After only squeaking by in his 1944 election, Taft won by more than 400,000 votes in 1950, the largest margin of any Senate race in state history to that point.[5]

Despite the labor resources poured into the contest, it was Taft, never a great campaigner, who appeared more successful in reaching out to workers. He shook hands with workers at factories across the state and made the CIO-PAC a key campaign topic. Taft won all the large industrial counties, even Cuyahoga. While workers briefly shut down a boiler room at Youngstown Sheet and Tube to protest Taft's visit on the campaign trail, the precincts immediately surrounding the plant shifted their voting from strong support for Truman (56 percent) in the 1948 presidential election to heavy Taft support (63 percent) for Senate two years later.[6] Afterward, Taft boasted that a "campaign based only on labor union appeal invites opposition and defeat." Samuel Lubell described the election as a rebuke of union leaders, arguing that "many workers seized upon Taft's candidacy to voice a protest against their own union chiefs." It was an embarrassment. Ohio unions were unable to mobilize their membership to vote on a clear-cut labor issue.[7]

Taft's campaign manager that year was Ray Bliss. As state Republican Party chair, Bliss led a highly resourceful organization in the 1950s. Bliss became the national party chairman in 1965. The party was centered in Cincinnati where it controlled 2,500 county and courthouse jobs "from which it obtained about $200,000 yearly in the form of a 2.5 percent 'voluntary contribution.'" The city machine, which dominated the state party, was also important nationally and had close business ties. Even union leaders in Cincinnati tended to be Republican or saw little to gain by working with Democrats. By maximizing its votes in rural areas, Cincinnati, and smaller cities, and by keeping issues which might arouse urban and working-class voters out of statewide campaigns, Bliss helped keep Ohio mostly in Republican control. While right-to-work and other anti-union bills were introduced multiple times in the state legislature during the 1950s, they never gained much traction. This was partly because Bliss and the Republican Party leadership never got behind them nor made it a focus for statewide candidates. This strategy appeared to pay off. In 1956, the Teamsters and the Ohio State Federation of Labor (OSFL) endorsed Republican William O'Neill in the governor's race over Toledo mayor Michael DiSalle.[8]

Like Indiana then, Ohio had a conservative lean by the 1950s. Unions in Ohio, like their counterparts to the west, were shut out of party politics in significant ways. However, the context of the 1958 campaign differed in at least a few important ways from Indiana a year before. First, right-to-work was put on the ballot in a consequential election year. Conservative stalwart John Bricker was up for reelection in the Senate as was incumbent Republican governor William O'Neill. Campaigning for governor two decades earlier, Bricker was happy to blast unions as "selfish" and not having the "interest of Ohio and all its citizens at heart." By 1958, and with unions more stable and far less radical, the senior senator saw little to gain by taking this route. Bricker and O'Neill were both supportive of right-to-work in principle; neither wanted to be the face of the issue. This proved to be a consistent source of tension between party leaders and the business activists behind the campaign. While the tepid support of key politicians seemed to favor labor, some of the more incendiary revelations of union corruption from the McClellan Committee hearings were just becoming public as the right-to-work campaign took off. Hearings picked up in the summer and fall of 1957, and the committee released its first report in the spring of 1958. Reports of union malfeasance and violence convinced many business leaders that the time was ripe to target unions. A final significant difference from prior campaigns is that the worst recession in two decades was beginning to wreak havoc on the industrial Midwest. The campaign would be fought in a climate of increasing economic anxiety.

Union and Employer Organization

Unions had a strong footing in the state by the mid-twentieth century, particularly in manufacturing. The state benefitted from the more than eighteen billion dollars pumped into war industries in the 1940s. More than 40 percent of workers were employed in manufacturing, and there were about a million union members in the state, covering 38 percent of all workers. Union security clauses were the norm in collective bargaining contracts. The wages of production workers were well above the national average due in part to the generous industry-wide contracts negotiated by the large industrial unions.[9]

There were traditional craft-industrial divides in the Ohio labor movement, and business leaders were quick to play up on them. The rival state labor federations did not merge until the spring of 1958. A fistfight even broke out at one of the OSFL's strategy meetings in the lead-up to the merger. That said, union divisions were subdued during the campaign compared to the acrimony in Indiana. All of the big unions save for the Teamsters made significant contributions. OSFL secretary treasurer Phil Hannah from the Machinists was friendly and occasionally worked with his CIO counterpart John Rooney and later Elmer Cope from the steelworkers. OSFL president Michael Lyden, the elder statesman of the Ohio labor movement, had stood with the Little Steel strikers in Youngstown in 1937 and did not harbor strong resentment toward the CIO like many AFL leaders. The two federations agreed to elect Lyden as the first president of the merged federation despite the larger share of CIO-affiliated union members in the state.[10]

Another difference in organization from prior campaigns is that, by 1958, right-to-work was a national issue. For the first time since the issue took off in the early 1940s, the national labor movement took a vested interest and provided organizational and strategic support to the Ohio labor movement. Ohio employers were also well organized at the start. National money and organizational support poured in on both sides. The Ohio Chamber of Commerce had experience in prior ballot initiatives and spearheaded the campaign. While Big Auto and Steel remained on the sidelines, this time several large *Fortune 500* manufacturers took an active interest in right-to-work, headed by General Electric and by former NAM president and ARMCO Steel executive Charles Hook.[11]

The arena of the ballot initiative meant that each side needed to build a stand-alone campaign organization and not only turn out their own supporters but also convey the importance of the issue to others beyond their close constituencies. This posed significant challenges for each side. Prior attempts by Ohio unions to engage just their members to vote on labor issues had failed. The business community in Ohio had close ties to a well-organized Republican Party which dominated the legislature. For the most part, however, party officials saw little upside in right-to-work. The state GOP succeeded in part by minimizing controversial issues that might increase voter turnout.

The Right-to-Work Campaign

The Ohio Chamber of Commerce began seriously hashing out a right-to-work plan in the fall of 1957 and pledged their formal support for the campaign at their October meeting in Columbus. Chamber leaders were no doubt energized by the right-to-work victory in neighboring Indiana and by the revelations of union corruption coming out of the McClellan Committee. William Presser, president of the Ohio Conference of Teamsters, was grilled by the committee and eventually charged with obstruction of justice for destroying union records subpoenaed by the committee. There were other local developments that inspired what in retrospect appeared to be an irrational confidence on the part of business. Just two years earlier, the labor movement was embarrassed in a ballot initiative for expanded unemployment insurance. The UAW and eventually other industrial unions negotiated industry-wide contracts that provided supplemental unemployment benefits (SUBs) for laid-off workers to help make up the difference between their normal pay and state-administered unemployment insurance. Some criticized the practice as double-dipping. The state legislature failed to affirm SUBs, so in 1955, the Ohio CIO took the proactive step to sponsor a ballot initiative explicitly allowing for SUBs and to raise the maximum unemployment insurance benefits for all workers. The Ohio Chamber of Commerce organized a front group in opposition, the Ohio Information Committee (named to reverse the CIO's initials). With organization in every county, the OIC helped to crush the ballot measure by a whopping 600,000 votes.

After shellacking labor, the Ohio Chamber's executive director Herschel Atkinson was the feature of a *U.S. News & World Report* article, "How to Beat Unions at the Polls," and his story was made into a widely circulated Chamber of Commerce pamphlet. Atkinson stressed the need to start early and to put forward a united business front to combat unions. Perhaps even more important, Atkinson and the OIC made the issue about union leaders and Walter Reuther in particular. OIC claimed that the labor-sponsored initiative attempted to subvert the decisions of a democratically elected legislature. Atkinson framed the issue as " 'The Legislature vs. the CIO'—NOT Business vs. Labor."[12]

With some minor tinkering, Atkinson believed business leaders could use this basic model with the infrastructure of the Ohio Chamber of Commerce, the in-house public relations office along with the reach of its affiliates in local communities, to make a public case for right-to-work. After all, business leaders in Indiana had taken a similar approach the year before.

A polling of Chamber members showed unanimous support for right-to-work and more than three-quarters believed that it would pass in Ohio if put up to a public vote. Sharing this confidence and central to the campaign were Charles Hook and Fred Lazarus. Lazarus helped build a retail empire in the 1920s by bringing Bloomingdale's and Filene's under the roof of Federated Department stores. He remained chairman of the board of Federated in the 1950s and was president of the Ohio Council of Retail Merchants. Hook headed the Cincinnati sheet metal producer ARMCO steel and had served as president of the NAM during the turbulent 1930s.[13] Together they were critical in pushing other business leaders to support right-to-work when Republican Party leadership wavered. Several large *Fortune 500* manufacturers also supported the Chamber's front group OHRTW. Business leaders in the state sent mailers to their employees on the issue and pushed reluctant political officials behind the scenes. Some took more visible roles. Notoriously anti-union Timken Roller Bearing took out full-page newspaper ads in support of right-to-work. Former state representative and central Ohio grain dealer Elton Kile chaired OHRTW. Following the Indiana model, proponents formed the Ohio Labor Committee for Right to Work as a stand-alone organization of dissident unionists, again headed by a former railroad conductor, S. D. Cadwallader of Toledo. The committee coordinated letters to the editor in state newspapers in support of right-to-work and distributed promotional materials, but otherwise remained in the background.

Unions came together quickly. In November 1957, officials from the OSFL, the state CIO council, the mine workers, and railroad brotherhoods formed a steering committee on right-to-work and eventually the stand-alone campaign organization United Organized Labor of Ohio (UOLO). UOLO was chaired by Ohio radio personality and former president of the American Federation of Television and Radio Artists Walter Davis. While the OSFL and state CIO council would not merge until May 1958, early union participation in UOLO was strong across craft and industrial unions.[14] For the first time, the AFL-CIO also took an active role. The AFL-CIO's Industrial Union Department (IUD) headed by Walter Reuther devoted an office to right-to-work, providing funding and assisting state affiliates with strategy. Reuther began to take a more serious interest in right-to-work when the NRTWC began putting up billboards in his home state of Michigan the year before. The involvement of national organizations on both sides made 1958 the most expensive ballot initiative and off-year election in Ohio history. Reports to the secretary of state place labor-side expenditures at just over a million dollars and business at just under, but these figures likely underestimate the totals on both sides. Business groups also had the free editorial support of the major newspapers in the state; 85 percent of the right-to-work editorials in Ohio papers were in favor of the issue.[15]

Proponents needed to collect more than 350,000 signatures with significant representation from at least half of Ohio's eighty-eight counties to put right-to-work on the ballot. When volunteers went out to collect signatures, they were often confronted by union members who urged them not to do so. In March, the labor paper *The Cleveland Union Leader* published the names of several Cleveland residents who had signed the petition, which prompted grumbles from the Chamber over "veiled intimidation." Unions fired back that it was employers who coerced their employees to sign and circulate petitions at work. In the end, the Chamber was forced to hire college students to finish the petition gathering, but it still secured 100,000 more signatures than they needed by the August 5 deadline.[16]

The Chamber of Commerce and OHRTW initially cast the debate in the familiar terms of freedom of choice. Chamber head Herschel Atkinson believed this best captured "the central ideas of voluntarism vs. compulsion in union membership" and OHRTW flyers emphasized their efforts to "protect a fundamental freedom . . . the right of free choice in union membership."[17] The union response was different from prior campaigns in at least a few ways. In April 1958, UOLO hired Charles Baker and Burr Public Relations to help craft their outreach strategy. Baker was from Toledo and had worked with the UAW in the past. At their first meeting, UOLO and Burr vowed not to go on the defensive and instead to make a positive case for labor. This approach was bolstered by the involvement of Reuther and the IUD. The IUD sponsored a spring conference on right-to-work strategy. Here Reuther argued that "it would be a tragic, tactical mistake to fight the 'right to work' conspiracy on a purely negative, defensive basis. We must make the fight on a positive basis . . . Talk the issues; talk aid to education, social security, housing; put these basic issues into their right relationship to the 'right to work' forces."[18]

For Baker, the first practical task was to sell UOLO to Ohio labor unions and rank-and-file members and to convince them that it was more than a "letterhead" organization. The second task was to build community coalitions. Baker and UOLO estimated that it would take at least a million votes from outside of union households to defeat right-to-work and pushed outreach from the beginning. By working with churches and other "good association" groups, they bet that unions could expand their reach while also benefitting from the greater legitimacy accorded to these groups.[19]

Particularly important were the major religious bodies of the state. Reverend Francis Carney of Cleveland repeatedly called right-to-work immoral in public statements. The Ohio Catholic Welfare Council (OCWC) came out against right-to-work in mid-March. OCWC secretary James Hollern gave speeches on the issue to church groups throughout the campaign. The OCWC anti-right-to-work resolution was followed by the General Assembly of Ohio Churches, the Ohio Conference of the African Methodist Episcopal Zion Church, and the rabbis of major Cleveland and Toledo synagogues. UOLO then tailored the statements of religious officials for different denominations so that volunteers could hand out materials after attending services. While the CIO had sought stronger ties with religious groups since the 1940s, their role in right-to-work campaigns amounted mostly to campaign literature. In Ohio, Baker hoped that more vocal religious support would provide a moral buffer of sorts from the sensational allegations of union corruption aired in the McClellan Committee hearings. It also put right-to-work proponents into the uncomfortable position of discrediting well-respected religious figures when advocating against their recommendations.[20]

UOLO also recruited several civic and fraternal organizations and encouraged them to issue statements in support of labor and drew up resolutions to take to their membership. These included the Knights of Columbus, Disabled American Veterans, and the Fraternal Order of Eagles. The NAACP came out against right-to-work at their national conference held in Cleveland in July followed by the Ohio state chapter in the fall. Thirty-three city councils had passed resolutions against right-to-work by October.[21]

Ohio Chamber of Commerce head Herschel Atkinson struggled to cultivate both new and familiar allies alike. He initially saw union workers as a potential source of support. One of the lessons he took from the 1955 defeat of the CIO-backed SUBs initiative was that "workers do not blindly follow union leaders in political affairs." But the Ohio Labor Committee for Right-to-Work never took off like he hoped. Both sides dismissed it as mostly a paper organization.[22] The Ohio Farm Bureau remained neutral, departing from the National Farm Bureau's pro-right-to-work position. More troubling, local chambers of commerce proved unreliable in carrying out campaign activities. OHRTW was counting on the infrastructure of the Chamber of Commerce to carry out the campaign as they had in the SUBs contest in 1955. This time the Cleveland Chamber of Commerce did not offer any formal endorsement of right-to-work while other local chambers were slow to help. As a result, OHRTW never built strong local committees outside of Cincinnati and Columbus. The business campaign was also missing one of its better organizers. Fred Milligan, the Columbus attorney and head of the OIC, was occupied fighting legal challenges to the unemployment system and only offered a passing endorsement for right-to-work.[23]

The other problem for right-to-work forces was getting the Republican Party establishment on board. For the first half of 1958, most politicians remained quiet on the issue. Bricker had received some assurance from Atkinson that the vote would be pushed back to 1959 after his election. The two were fairly close. As governor, he appointed his friend "Hirsch" as director of unemployment compensation and later recommended him for the leadership position with the Chamber. Party chairman Ray Bliss worked hard behind the scenes to delay the vote for fear of sabotaging the Republican ticket. By the summer, however, business leaders were more strident in their push for right-to-work. This came to a head in Cincinnati in July, just weeks before the deadline to submit right-to-work petitions to the secretary of state. Charles Hook called for a secret meeting of top right-to-work backers in the business community as well as select Republican politicians at the exclusive Queen City Club. The participants give a window into right-to-work support that is not visible from campaign speeches and advertisements. In addition to the core three of Atkinson, Hook, and Lazarus, the thirty some odd executives in the room included Proctor & Gamble president Howard Morgens, executives from Standard Oil, Champion Paper, General Electric, Eagle-Pitcher, Youngstown Sheet and Tube, and Timken Roller Bearing. Despite the absence of the big automakers, there was a significant push from large corporations. At least eight *Fortune 500* firms, five of them in the top 150, backed OHRTW.[24]

At the meeting, Bricker was in disbelief as the business leaders made the case for the ballot initiative. He even pleaded that right-to-work would bring a union landslide big enough to propel his opponent, the perennial and mostly unsuccessful Democratic candidate Stephen Young, into office. This prompted laughter from some of the executives. Most of them saw little threat from any of the Democratic candidates for statewide office. Led by Hook, they were convinced that the public was ready to curb unions and they pushed forward. It was only after the petitions were submitted and after more pressure from the business community that Bricker begrudgingly came around to right-to-work.[25]

This left Bricker, incumbent governor William O'Neill, and conservative Democratic Senator Frank Lausche (who was not up for reelection) as the most high-profile politicians in favor of right-to-work. After the summer meeting in Cincinnati, O'Neill increasingly rebranded his election campaign as a crusade for right-to-work.[26] As an easy-going, moderate Republican in the Eisenhower mold, O'Neill seemed a peculiar right-to-work champion. He was a far cry from Bricker or union antagonists on the national scene like Barry Goldwater. By the 1956 governor's race, he was seen as a potential national star. He was the youngest ever speaker of the house at thirty and was elected attorney general at thirty-four in 1950. Labor was not a theme in his 1956 campaign for governor—he received the endorsement of the state federation of labor—when he comfortably defeated DiSalle. It was not until his administration got off to a slow start in 1957, and after he was effectively sidelined for months in the beginning of 1958 after suffering a mild heart attack, that O'Neill became more receptive to right-to-work.

While O'Neill and Bricker eventually came around to embrace right-to-work, the national Republican establishment never really did. President Eisenhower did not come to Ohio to campaign on behalf of Republican candidates. Worse, his secretary of labor James Mitchell publicly questioned the sense of right-to-work initiatives in an appearance on ABC's *Open Hearing* show. In a letter to President Eisenhower, Charles Hook bemoaned the "terrible wallop" that the secretary's comments had inflicted on the campaign.[27]

Notably, Republicans were not the only ones seeking to avoid labor. If asked, Democratic gubernatorial candidate Michael DiSalle stated his opposition to right-to-work but refused to make it a campaign issue. Instead, he went the other way and proposed anti-racketeering reforms and accused O'Neill of backroom deals with Ohio Teamsters' leader Bill Presser. DiSalle claimed to have returned all of his union campaign contributions to avoid any hint of corruption.[28]

Heading into the fall, everything still pointed to a close race. An August poll contracted by UOLO showed 31 percent clearly against right-to-work, 29 percent for it, and the remaining 40 percent undecided. A Harris and Associates poll conducted in early September revealed a similarly even split with a large share of undecided voters. By October, bookies on Vincent Street in Cleveland were offering 7 to 5 odds that right-to-work would pass.[29] In the last few months of the campaign, each side amped up its advertising and outreach efforts. In a letter to UAW director of public relations Frank Winn at the end of September, Charles Baker noted his pleasure with UOLO's rank-and-file involvement. Four thousand union supporters turned out for a September rally in Columbus and took more than a million pieces of literature back to their communities. Union members' demand for bumper stickers literally ran the state out of bumper sticker paper, leaving candidates for office waiting on a refill. Baker and UOLO were also pleasantly surprised by the voter registration efforts in the larger cities.[30]

Labor's big challenge was to separate the right-to-work issue from allegations of union corruption. Less than a month before the election *U.S. News & World Report* ran a feature on the findings of the McClellan Committee hearings. The cover story, "Can the Labor Racketeer Be Stopped?," featured a lengthy interview with Senator McClellan. Case histories inside highlighted the most sordid details of bombings, sabotage, and intimidation dug up by the committee. UOLO encouraged members to emphasize the overwhelming support of clergy for the union side when separating incidents of union corruption from the larger aims of right-to-work supporters.[31] Organizers also warned unions to guard against any last-minute incidents of strike violence or intimidation to avoid any October Surprise that could turn the public against them.

By October, OHRTW clearly saw the corruption angle as their best strategy and went all in. O'Neill was particularly vocal. In a televised address shortly before the election, he stressed union corruption and the Teamsters in particular:

> I am for the right-to-work amendment because I want to protect the union member from the corrupt labor bosses and give the union member some weapon with which to fight corruption and oppression in his union . . . This man—James Hoffa—is the national dictator of the Teamsters Unions, with final and absolute control over all members of the teamster unions in Ohio . . . Tomorrow, by lifting his voice, he can stop the delivery of bread, milk, newspapers and a hundred other products.[32]

Pro-right-to-work materials went much further. A front-page ad in the *Canton Repository* warned readers that "Jimmy Hoffa Will Get You If You Don't Watch Out for Your Right to Work." An OHRTW brochure targeting women cast right-to-work as a fight against fear, a vote to protect their husbands and children from corrupt union bosses and labor violence. One television ad featured a threatening figure, the stereotypical "union boss," warning viewers not to vote for the amendment. Another ad featured clips of a Cecil DeMille film showing mob violence and cars being overturned.[33] O'Neill's more strident attack on labor drew cheers from many business leaders, but the focus on corruption appeared to have some limits.[34] Several stations stopped running the DeMille ad after church groups complained.[35]

On Election Day, the right-to-work amendment lost by a landslide, nearly two-to-one. It was soundly defeated even in some of the most rural counties. In the end, seventy-two of eighty-eight Ohio counties voted against right-to-work. The heavy voter turnout bolstered by UOLO's registration drives and their get-out-the-vote operation did not bode well for conservative candidates. It was the biggest turnout for a midterm election to date, even exceeding the 1956 presidential election. William O'Neill lost to his 1956 opponent Michael DiSalle. In the most stunning development, John Bricker lost his reelection bid to perennial candidate Stephen Young. Bricker privately attributed his defeat to the recklessness of business leaders at their July meeting in Cincinnati. Bliss was more candid. Shortly after the vote he told the press that he "repeatedly warned proponents of this issue that this defeat would be a possible consequence," but that "they chose to ignore my warnings."[36]

Union Outreach and the Right-to-Work Vote

The labor campaign in Ohio differed from prior efforts in two important ways. First, union divisions were mostly muted. UOLO secured the participation of most Ohio unions well before the merger of the OSFL and state CIO in the spring. Second, both national and state labor organizations committed resources early and worked with public relations and outreach specialists to develop a sophisticated campaign organization. Together, this aided union member mobilization and, importantly, the formation of a broader coalition and more compelling framing of right-to-work. The coalition removed labor leaders as the face of the campaign. It was this wider reach and more positive face that helped unions flip the script in Ohio. In comparison, the business campaign quickly splintered such that it was limited to an insular group of business leaders at the end. This, too, was partly due to labor pressure, which dissuaded likely business allies to come on board.

Later I detail the changes in member mobilization and union outreach that were critical for the campaign. First, it is worth noting that nothing suggested a union landslide or even a likely union victory at the outset. Political opportunities were mixed. While key Republicans like Bricker and O'Neill were slow to come around to right-to-work in an election year, revelations of union corruption streaming in from the McClellan Committee soured many on labor and led key business leaders to conclude that the time was now to push for restrictions on unions. Polling in the fall showed the public evenly split on right-to-work.[37] Moreover, organizations on both sides appeared well-equipped at the outset and both poured considerable resources into the campaign. The more wide-open setting would seemingly favor large membership organizations like labor unions over business groups. Yet, prior to the 1958 campaign, there was no reason to suspect that Ohio unions, however large and resourceful, were up to the task. Only three years earlier, the Ohio Chamber of Commerce and their OIC front group helped to crush the CIO-sponsored initiative on SUBs. The year 1958 turned into a Democratic one, as I return to later, but even here, Ohio stood out.

What changed for labor in Ohio? Craft-industrial divisions were not absent, but they did not shape the campaign. Instead, the buy-in of most unions to the UOLO campaign organization ensured a united front throughout. The threat of right-to-work hastened merger negotiations and both craft and industrial unions contributed immediately to UOLO, months before the merger. Even before the Chamber's push on right-to-work, the building trades softened their opposition to the merger of the state federations. The hastening of labor unity was driven in part by the real threat of right-to-work post-Indiana and to the diligence of UOLO. The biggest contributions to UOLO came from a handful of unions representing both federations including the UAW, Carpenters, Machinists, Steelworkers, and the UMW. In all, more than 1,300 local unions, nearly a quarter of all locals in the state, committed one dollar per member to the campaign. This is all to say that divisions did not approach the dysfunctional status of Indiana, and they were mostly under the radar. The only noticeable split during the right-to-work campaign was due to the expulsion of the Teamsters from the AFL-CIO the year before.[38]

The widespread buy-in by union locals spurred considerable participation by union members. There are no hard figures on union member participation in the campaign, but anecdotal data show why Charles Baker and UOLO were pleased with the effort by early fall. Seventeen distribution centers were set up across the state for pamphlets and outreach guides. Labor committees were organized in every county. UOLO sold out of anti-right-to-work bumper stickers. Local unions ran ads signed by members in more than one hundred newspapers across the state in the final months. Efforts to register union members to vote also appeared effective. Of the nineteen most populous counties, all but two saw an increase in registration from the presidential election of 1956 to the 1958 midterms, reversing the typical pattern.[39]

The second defining element of the labor campaign was its sophistication. The stand-alone campaign organization UOLO got an early start, they worked with public relations specialists, and they tailored materials to important demographics. Here they benefitted from a good bit of organizing and political capital among the state labor movement. Vice president of the newly merged state AFL-CIO Phil Hannah was an assistant secretary of labor in the Truman administration. Secretary treasurer Elmer Cope was a Swarthmore-educated labor progressive. He had taken classes at Brookwood Labor College before joining SWOC in the thirties and saw coalitions and outreach as central. This was all bolstered by the support of national labor movement and Walter Reuther and the AFL-CIO's IUD in particular.

Both UOLO and Reuther pushed to develop a more positive message on labor and right-to-work. It is notable that here both labor and liberal strategists saw gain in removing unions, and especially union leaders, from the forefront. This was an early focus of UOLO in forming ties with "good association groups," particularly clergy, and it was reiterated at key points in the campaign. In August 1958, Roy Reuther, the head of the UAW Citizenship Department, wrote to his brother Walter warning him of the danger of emphasizing labor too much: "Labor may well be falling into a trap of the opposition by making the 'right-to-work' issue the primary or exclusive issue in the fall elections. It is my feeling that we can mobilize far more public and rank and file labor support in opposition to right-to-work legislation if we tie it in with an issue that has wider public interest and support."[40]

The September Ohio report by Louis Harris & Associates was more pointed:

> It is undoubtedly best for the burden of right to work to be carried not by a publicity campaign waged by a trade union group which cuts itself off from the rest of the community, but rather by a series of local or regional committees across the state. This can be done by getting many citizens who surely must be against this measure (such as clergymen, educators, and

others) to sponsor locally whatever publicity is gotten out . . . the measure should be tied to the recession and the main stream of the issues that are on people's minds. Otherwise, the electorate will be forced into a simply pro- or anti-union vote, which might not turn out the right way.[41]

The ad in Figure 4.1 is one such publicity attempt by a loosely affiliated community group. Unions are not mentioned in the many groups opposed to right-to-work, or anywhere for that matter. Part of tying right-to-work to the "main stream" of issues on people's minds was connecting labor to the mainstream in the first place. UOLO secured the support and participation of rank-and-file workers, as noted earlier, but also civic groups and the major religious bodies of the state. Without this, there was not much confidence in liberal and labor

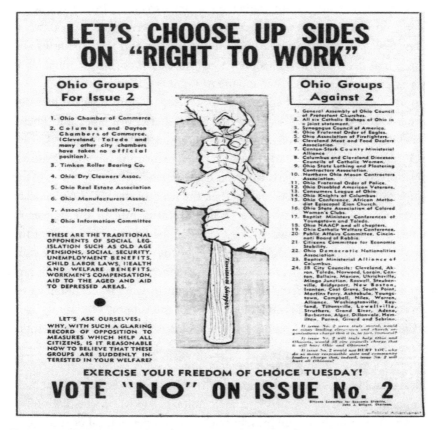

Figure 4.1 Community Groups against Right-to-Work

Note: Ad placed by John J. Gilligan and the Citizens Committee for Economic Stability in the *Cincinnati Enquirer*, October 30, 1958, p. 23. Courtesy of Susan Fremont.

circles on the outcome of a simple up or down vote on the merits of unions. Polling before and after the election suggests that this kind of union outreach and messaging was effective in connecting beyond labor's base. Understanding of right-to-work increased from 58 percent to 76 percent. Aside from businessmen, every other demographic showed a significant drop in support for right-to-work, even among professionals (down 10 percent from a few months before the election) and white-collar employees (down 8 percent). Whereas the 1955 campaign against SUBs effectively isolated union leaders from the rest of the community, this time UOLO was successful in connecting unions to other more respected community partners.[42]

Variation across counties offers another window into labor outreach. To understand how labor fared in more or less favorable contexts, I conducted supplemental regression analyses across counties. Not surprisingly, the pro-labor vote share (the percentage voting against right-to-work) is lower in conservative counties that voted for Eisenhower at higher rates than their peers two years earlier, while counties with larger Catholic populations exhibited higher pro-labor voting. More telling, however, is the comparison between right-to-work and the ill-fated labor initiative on unemployment insurance in 1955 (SUBs). In the 1955 ballot initiative, the labor side lost by more than 600,000 votes, with eighty-one of eighty-eight counties voting against it. Of these eighty-one counties, labor was successful in getting sixty-five to switch over and vote against right-to-work three years later. The switchover counties look like the rest of the state for the most part; UOLO was able to reach *average* Ohio counties that had proven elusive in prior years.[43]

The business effort was the mirror opposite in some respects, marked both by division and limited outreach. Atkinson, Hook, and Lazarus pushed ahead with the campaign without strong local commitment or the support of their most likely allies. Most surprisingly, many local chambers of commerce did not actively support the campaign, particularly in heavily unionized areas. Republican officials like Bliss never warmed to it, while Bricker and O'Neill only did so begrudgingly. When asked about the lopsided right-to-work defeat, Fred Milligan, the Columbus lawyer and OIC head from the SUBs campaign, lamented the limited business outreach: "labor had grassroots; the Chamber had none." This did not happen in a vacuum. Union supporters challenged petitioners early on. UOLO encouraged union members to avoid businesses that supported right-to-work. They secured the support of major religious bodies in the spring and summer. Union voter registration efforts were also showing promising returns by the summer. It was in this context of considerable labor activity that Milligan notes how "[T]he Chambers of Commerce weren't able to get people to stick their necks out."[44]

The limited outreach meant that OHRTW did not span much farther than the core group of business leaders and a handful of politicians. The labor committee for right-to-work was mostly invisible. Whereas UOLO had information distribution centers across the state and local committees in every county, local right-to-work organization was limited beyond Cincinnati, Dayton, and Columbus. More than 80 percent of the OHRTW budget was devoted to media. The sparse participation of not only ordinary workers, but credible organizations beyond the business community, made it difficult to communicate any bigger public stake in the issue. Some of the most visible employers in the campaign (e.g., Timken) were also notoriously anti-union, opening up the campaign to criticism of being self-serving and overreaching. By the end of the campaign, OHRTW, dominated by the core business leaders and without the support of the GOP establishment, focused almost entirely on the sensational details of union corruption from the McClellan Committee. Cut off from key political allies, this was perhaps the most sensible route for OHRTW at the end, but it had clear limits.

There were of course other factors at work in 1958 besides labor outreach. For one, it turned into a Democratic year and the recession took a heavy toll across the Midwest. Right-to-work was voted down in five other states and Democrats took control of Congress. Yet Ohio still stands out. Nearly 54 percent of gubernatorial voters in nonsouthern states went Democratic in 1958, while in Ohio this inched closer to 57 percent. More telling is the swing from the previous election. The Democratic swing in gubernatorial voting between 1956 and 1958 was plus 22.76 percent in Ohio versus plus 8 percent in both nonsouthern states generally and Midwestern states in particular; Democratic congressional voting was plus 16 percent in Ohio versus plus 10 percent in both nonsouthern states generally and the Midwest in particular.[45]

Moreover, in the industrial Midwest, blame for the recession was up for debate for most of late 1957 and 1958. Whether one saw it as the "Reuther recession" or blamed the Eisenhower administration was not always predictable outside of core business and union circles. As Donald Stokes described, "[R]esponsibility for the economic distress of 1957–1958 was not at first charged to the business community . . . it was not until right-to-work was brought before the public that the economic distress was given a forceful political translation." As this chapter has shown, such a forceful political translation took considerable effort on the part of labor as well as a change in approach from prior years.[46]

The Aftermath

The fallout of the 1958 elections was significant in Ohio and beyond. The Ohio Republican ticket was a disaster as Ray Bliss had feared. Democrat Michael DiSalle was elected governor and Democrats gained control of both chambers of the state legislature. Ohio AFL-CIO secretary treasurer Elmer Cope saw this as the moment to make up for a lost decade in the legislature. Unions made gains in this more favorable context, though they were uneven. The 1959 legislature finally authorized SUBs and passed a Fair Employment Practices law. At the same time, it failed to act on minimum wage or repeal the prohibition on public-sector organizing. DiSalle remained ambivalent toward the labor movement. While he supported union activist Frank King for Senate Majority Leader, he used his first state of the state address to push for reforms addressing union corruption. He twice lobbied the House Judiciary Committee on an anti-racketeering bill only to see it narrowly voted down on the House floor.[47]

Elsewhere, the overreach of business leaders and political hopefuls likewise cost Republicans. Harold Handley lost in his 1958 campaign for US Senate in Indiana. In California, conservative and right-to-work supporter William Knowland lost in his bid for governor. The immediate result for the right-to-work movement was a scaling back of activity in the industrial Midwest. In Illinois, some Republican legislators had sought to put right-to-work on the ballot as a legislative initiative in 1957 but eyed 1959 as a more realistic opportunity. This ground to a halt after the sizeable defeat in Ohio. In May 1958, the Wisconsin Republican Party convention voted to push the 1959 legislature to order a state-wide referendum on right-to-work.[48] This too fizzled after the election. Instead, long dormant progressive policies gained some traction.

Conclusion

Given the lopsided labor victory, the confidence of business leaders like Charles Hook and Fred Lazarus appears foolhardy in retrospect. Yet they were not alone in thinking this was *the* time to curb unions. Labor unions in Ohio had shown nothing in the decade to indicate they were capable of mobilizing their own members on labor issues, not to mention broader constituencies. National press coverage of the labor movement was dominated by allegations of corruption from the McClellan Committee. Public opinion on right-to-work appeared split into the fall. But unions helped to turn the outcome into a rout. With divisions muted, and considerable campaign expertise at their disposal, UOLO got significant rank-and-file participation, formed a wide-ranging coalition, and moved away from a purely defensive approach to right-to-work. This outsider route to success was based in part on making right-to-work less of a labor issue and removing union leaders as its public face. The more positive face and message on right-to-work was made possible by the surprisingly broad coalition. The Chamber of Commerce and OHRTW lacked both united business participation and credible allies. In the more wide-open format of the ballot initiative, they failed to keep pace with the union effort in a major reversal from the SUBs effort just three years earlier.

5

The Insider Route in Wisconsin

As right-to-work campaigns were heating up in the Midwest, public-sector union advocates in Wisconsin were waging an uphill, mostly under-the-radar battle for state recognition. Public-sector workers and their fledgling unions were already making demands on their employers in big cities across the country with varying degrees of formality and success. In the Midwest, for example, Illinois authorized the Chicago Transit Authority to continue collective bargaining with transit workers after the authority became publicly owned in the 1940s. But no state or federal labor law gave public-sector workers affirmative rights to form unions or to force their employers to listen when they did. In this chapter, I trace the development of the first statewide public-sector bargaining legislation in Wisconsin in 1959 and the campaign waged by municipal employees there. The case for public-sector rights lacked the fanfare of the campaigns in Indiana and Ohio, though it was clearly shaped by the political winds surrounding these efforts. Indeed, well before the upsurge of civil rights–inspired public-sector organizing in the 1960s and 1970s, bargaining rights in Wisconsin were rooted in the 1950s fights over labor rights. It was after more than a decade of public-sector advocates organizing and introducing bills in the legislature, and after the overreach of business activists on right-to-work in the region, that dissension within the Republican Party and between party leaders and business circles provided the opening that activists needed.

The success of the public-sector union campaign in Wisconsin is mostly a story of political opportunity. The insider route pursued by public-sector union activists did not involve a wide-ranging coalition, many strikes, or much protest. It was under the radar even within the Wisconsin labor movement. Instead, it hinged on the slow cultivation of key political allies. The weakened state of both the Wisconsin Democratic Party and union political programs allowed savvy activists to forge union–party linkages without much resistance from entrenched interests—linkages that were strengthened as the party moved from a sometimes third-place finisher in state politics to a major force.

Heartland Blues. Marc Dixon, Oxford University Press (2020). © Oxford University Press.
DOI: 10.1093/oso/9780190917036.001.0001.

After governor Gaylord Nelson signed the nation's first statewide public-sector bargaining statute in 1959, the Wisconsin Council of County and Municipal Employees (WCCME) cheered the new legislation as the beginning of an "enlightened era" of collective bargaining. This proved overly optimistic, but the Wisconsin effort provided a model for the only union growth over the second half of the twentieth century. Campaigns following Wisconsin had a harder time flying under the radar as public-sector labor rights became a more visible and hotly contested issue. I return to these latter developments in the region, as well as the slowdown in right-to-work activism, in the next chapter.

I begin this chapter by describing the political opportunities, the status of unions, public-sector workers, and business opposition in Wisconsin in the mid-twentieth century and how it differs from the other campaign states. After providing an account of the legislative push for public-sector collective bargaining rights, I assess the role of key union activists in forging party linkages and the political opportunities that accelerated their efforts at the end of the decade.

Wisconsin in the 1950s

Wisconsin had settled on a conservative political course in the 1940s and 1950s, though it was the legacy of progressivism and its eventual fallout that laid the groundwork for the labor–Democratic Party ties and the push for public-sector collective bargaining rights. The Progressive movement brought a spate of reforms across the United States, and Wisconsin stands out in this regard. The state passed early civil service legislation, the nation's first Workers' Compensation law in 1911, and was a pioneer in child labor and safety laws as well as unemployment insurance. Academics, most notably John Commons and the "Wisconsin School," played a prominent role in the shaping of social reform in the state and nationally.[1]

Historically, support for progressive policies in Wisconsin was strongest in the largely Scandinavian counties in the northwest of the state as well as in Milwaukee. For a moment, however, it was widespread. The wave of discontent that ushered in "Fighting Bob" La Follette as governor in 1900 stemmed from the dominance and perceived malfeasance of the state's leading industries of the nineteenth century. Railroad and lumber interests often worked together and held sway over state government in a way not witnessed in Ohio and Indiana. Lacking the lush and fertile farmland of the Corn Belt states, Wisconsin offered no frontier outlet beyond the reach of these industries and was ripe for a more pronounced backlash to big business. Notably, however, this protest was carried out within the Wisconsin Republican Party. Between 1900 and 1934, the Republican Party was home to both La Follette progressives and socialists of various stripes as well as conservative Republicans in the national mold. Progressives built a separate party in the 1930s only to come back to the Republican Party in 1946. Behind these competing slates, Democrats were a weak second- or sometimes third-place finisher in state politics. For the first half of the century, then, the party was not a home for Wisconsin unions.[2]

The Decline of Progressivism and the Rise of Wisconsin Democrats

The progressive lineage of the state was in the rearview mirror by the early post–World War II years. The stand-alone Progressive Party began to falter in the early 1940s. The tipping point was in 1946 when Robert La Follette Jr. opted to run as a Republican instead of a Progressive in his reelection campaign for US Senate. Instead of reclaiming the party of his father, La Follette lost in the primary to a relative unknown in Joseph McCarthy. In a strange twist, La Follette lost Milwaukee County, a union hotbed. This was due in part to opposition from communist-dominated unions of the Milwaukee Industrial Union Council. The leftist faction of CIO unions headed by the UAW local at the giant Allis-Chalmers plant actively opposed La Follette for his isolationist stance and his critical statements on the Soviet Union. AFL unions from the Wisconsin State Federation of Labor (WSFL) did not offer any support and instead just encouraged their members to vote. The United Labor Committee that was hurried together to oppose McCarthy in the general election did not put up much of a fight, and he was easily elected.[3]

In the decade following World War II, Wisconsin was a mostly conservative, Republican-dominated state. The state legislature was controlled by Republicans. Voters elected Eisenhower at a 5 percent higher clip than the national average in 1952 and 1956. Walter Kohler, a moderate Republican in the Eisenhower mold, was a popular three-term governor. While Republicans went along with some business pushes to curb unions, as I describe later, it did not become a priority until the end of the decade when right-to-work gained steam in the region.[4]

Unions had few allies in the Wisconsin Republican Party of the 1940s and 1950s. With no clear home base, a small network of young progressives and labor activists turned to the Democratic Party, long an afterthought in Wisconsin politics and just a shell by the late 1940s. Some prominent party leaders in the state like Democratic national committee member Robert Tehan actively encouraged this takeover, while the older, more conservative faction offered little resistance. The takeover was formalized with the creation of the Democratic Organizing Committee (DOC) in 1948. Most of the young activists had worked together on Progressive Party campaigns at the University of Wisconsin in the late 1930s and early 1940s. One contrast to the patronage-oriented parties in Indiana and Ohio, which often kept unions at arm's length, is that Wisconsin union activists were critical to the building of the new Democratic Party. In building the party from scratch, DOC leaders would select a trusted person in an unorganized county, typically a unionist or a former Progressive, or both, to hold meetings and generate lists of supporters. Many individual unions, including nascent public-sector unions, began working with the party in the 1950s and were critical for its rise. Two figures in particular, labor lawyer John Lawton and his colleague and eventual governor and US Senator Gaylord Nelson, were central to both Democratic Party growth and public-sector bargaining legislation.[5]

Unions, Public-Sector Workers, and Employer Organization

The WSFL historically had strong socialist leadership out of Milwaukee. Henry Ohl of the Typographical workers and John Handley of the Machinists cut their teeth in Milwaukee's socialist government in the 1910s and were both strong organizers. The WSFL often worked with the La Follette wing of the Republican Party. The arrival of CIO unions in the late 1930s was headlined by UAW organizing victories in Milwaukee and the smaller industrial cities in southern Wisconsin, including big locals at Briggs and Stratton, General Motors, Harley-Davidson, and farm equipment manufacturer Allis-Chalmers. The industrial composition of the state made for a different mix of unions than in Indiana and Ohio. There were no basic steel plants in Wisconsin, and the USWA had a slower start as a result. Unions were strong in basic industry but also in meatpacking, brewing, and in the paper mills in the northern part of the state. The UAW was the largest union in the state followed by the Machinists.[6]

The biggest union divisions were not always between craft and industrial factions, but within the state CIO council, where leftists and centrists wrestled for control in an often public and messy contest. This culminated in a purge of leftist leadership first in the Milwaukee Industrial Union Council and then in the state council in late 1946. By the 1950s, 38 percent of Wisconsin workers belonged to unions, and there were twice as many AFL union members as CIO union members.[7]

The state AFL and CIO federations did not merge until July 1958, but union divisions did not play a critical role in the quest for public-sector collective bargaining rights. Rather, neither of the state federations, or even the AFL-CIO, paid much attention to public-sector workers for most of the decade. This limited standing of public-sector workers in the state labor movement was common across the industrial Midwest. At the dawn of the 1950s, the WSFL had become mostly apolitical under the leadership of George Haberman, save for perfunctory endorsements before elections. The state CIO, and its largest union in the UAW, were preoccupied with the long and ugly strike at the Kohler Company in Sheboygan. From 1954 through 1960 when the strike was called off, bitter resistance by the firm, violence on the picket line, and a national boycott against Kohler had nearly torn the town apart. When the McClellan Committee's young chief counsel Robert Kennedy arrived in Sheboygan in 1958, he found the town as deeply divided and the company as unyielding as union officials had warned.[8]

Business opposition to unions was led by the Wisconsin Chamber of Commerce and some of the more activist employers including Kohler, run by relatives of governor Walter Kohler, and Allen-Bradley in Milwaukee. Historically, Wisconsin employers were less active on state labor issues than their counterparts in Indiana and Ohio. This began to change in the mid-1950s as the Kohler conflict escalated and briefly ensnarled public-sector workers. Opposition to public-sector bargaining in particular came from the Chamber and the Wisconsin League of Municipalities.[9]

Public-sector workers were organizing and making demands on employers in the 1950s even if they were mostly an afterthought for the state federations. This, of course, was not new to the 1950s. Teacher associations emerged in the nineteenth century. The Progressive Era push for civil service reform bolstered public-sector organizing in the 1910s. The American Federation of State, County and Municipal Employees (AFSCME) formed in

Wisconsin in the 1930s. After World War II, it was common for local union officers in big cities to meet with administrators over wages and working conditions and even reach written agreements, if not the collective bargaining contracts private-sector unions would have recognized at that time. Cincinnati had bargained informally with AFSCME locals since the 1940s. Joseph Slater finds that by the late 1950s, nearly a third of AFSCME locals nationwide reached similar "agreements" with their employers and this was common across much of the Midwest.[10]

Wisconsin had a similar percentage of public-sector workers as its Midwestern neighbors. It boasted higher percentages of public workers in blue-collar positions such as highways and sanitation. By the 1950s, it also boasted considerable organizing and political advocacy relative to its neighbors, particularly Indiana. While AFSCME was organizing and engaging in informal bargaining in Ohio and Michigan as well, those states had adopted statutes restricting public-sector unions in 1947. The consistent legislative effort in Wisconsin was due in part to unusually resourceful local activists and their ties to the new Democratic Party.[11]

The Long Push for Public-Sector Labor Rights

The origins of public-sector unionism in Wisconsin predate the CIO and the New Deal. It began as a top-down bureaucratic arrangement. In the spring of 1932, Henry Ohl of the WSFL met with progressive Republican governor Philip La Follett and the state personnel administrator to discuss the idea of a union for state employees. Ohl and the WSFL had long-standing ties to the La Follettes and the progressive wing of the Republican Party. With the governor's blessing, the union formed as the Wisconsin State Association of Administrative, Clerical, Fiscal and Technical Employees. But La Follette lost in the primary that year and the state Civil Service System soon came under attack by the new legislature, an odd mix of Republicans and conservative Democrats. Led by its most active member, Arnold Zander, the fledgling union of about fifty members orchestrated a public relations campaign that helped to stave off the attack on the Civil Service system and solidify the new organization. In 1936, the union received a national charter from the AFL as the American Federation of State, County and Municipal Employees, with Zander as its president and its headquarters in Madison. It would remain there until 1957 when it moved to Washington.[12]

By the end of World War II, AFSCME organizations, led by its municipal affiliates under the WCCME, were becoming recognized in more or less formal ways in the state's urban centers. WCCME represented a mix of blue- and white-collar employees, including highway workers, police in Madison, and general office staff across the state. State employees instead pursued a lobbying strategy, pushing the legislature for paid holidays and sick leave. Led by Roy Kubista, a student of Social Security architect Edwin Witte at the University of Wisconsin, the Wisconsin State Employees Association helped create the state employees' pension system in the 1940s. Most often, they used the Civil Service system as a platform to engage state administrators.[13]

Outside of the major cities, the experiences of public-sector union activists varied wildly. Unions often struggled to make inroads in rural areas, and organizing efforts were easily stymied by the dismissal of union activists. Employer intransigence sparked two strikes by highway workers in Eau Claire during the 1950s. During this time, there was still debate within AFSCME on the merits of collective bargaining versus utilizing existing Civil Service frameworks to better working conditions. Some occupational groups eschewed collective bargaining and union rights. Teacher associations under the Wisconsin Educational Association Council, whose origins date to the nineteenth century, were still dominated by administrators and had yet to take on union functions.[14]

Amid these varied experiences and perspectives on unions, the push for collective bargaining rights emerges from the work of John Lawton and Gaylord Nelson and went hand in hand with the rebuilding of the Democratic Party.[15] Lawton, pictured in Figure 5.1, was the son of teachers, and Nelson the son of a country doctor; both were raised in Wisconsin families that voted for the La Follette slate in the Republican primary and Democrats for president. The two met in the Young Progressives at the University of Wisconsin and had hit the road together campaigning for Robert La Follette in 1940. After law school, Lawton started at the Dane County District Attorney's office, where the WCCME had just formed a local chapter. He was one of the first active members and was elected president. He took these union ties with him when he went into private practice, representing the Madison Federation of Labor, the Firefighters, and the WCCME. Nelson served as a lieutenant in the army during World War II. When he returned home in 1946, he promptly joined Lawton's firm in Madison.[16]

In 1951 Lawton and the WCCME sponsored 462-S, which granted municipal employees the right to organize. The bill was ambiguous when it came

Figure 5.1 John Lawton
Lawton at his Madison office in 1954. Photo courtesy of Wisconsin Historical Society.

to bargaining. It called for "collective considerations" between local units of government and their employees by allowing them to form and join labor unions of their own choosing and to encourage mutual understandings between the parties on issues of wages, hours, and other conditions of employment. Lawton presented this as a minor change in labor regulation and the bill did not garner much public interest. It nearly sneaked in under the radar in the Republican-dominated legislature. But the ambiguous bargaining language did not ease the fears of employers. Public and private employers drew on familiar arguments against organized government employees. The League of Municipalities correctly attacked it as being only an entering wedge, which would help set precedent and allow unions to build on these initial rights. They went on to suggest the bill would foment strikes and labor troubles. The League and many individual municipalities brought up the specter of police strikes and the inability of unionized police to keep the peace in industrial disputes.[17]

Lawton responded to the Senate Labor Committee that there had been no police strikes in Wisconsin and that the AFSCME constitution barred any of its local union affiliates representing protective service workers from striking. In making the case for public-sector union rights, he described public employees as lacking the basic rights and ability to protect themselves through organization that all other employees and even employers had. "Lawyers and doctors have their own organizations, which to a great extent are trade unions under another name. . . . Farmers belong to the Farm Bureau Federation. . . . Public employees at the level of state and local governments has as great a need for organization to which they seek to improve their conditions as any other group in our society." A watered-down version of the bill, which removed the language of collective considerations in favor of "promoting better understanding" between municipal employees and their employers, passed but was vetoed by moderate Republican governor Walter Kohler Jr.[18]

Generating support for public-sector bargaining and for Democrats more generally was slow. Nelson was elected to the Wisconsin State Senate in 1948. Early on there were not enough Democrats for him to get a second for a roll call as the floor leader. Establishing the party as the legitimate heir to the Progressives took time. As then DOC chair James Doyle quipped, "there are places around the state where it takes courage to be a Democrat." Nelson later described the situation of the early 1950s in a similar manner. "[T]he Democratic Party did not have good progressive credentials. If you were a liberal, you were with the La Follettes and Franklin Roosevelt." When leafleting plant gates at the paper mills upstate in the early 1950s, workers would see "Democrat" and throw it on the ground. But things did change and unions began to play a bigger role. After Lawton would get a labor-friendly bill introduced, he would present the roll call vote to his union clients as mounting evidence of labor's political problem. Many of them became active in the Democratic Party.[19]

If the legislative prospects for public-sector unions dimmed in the mid-1950s, contention over union rights heated up. Walter Kohler was easily reelected governor in 1952. In 1953, Republican attorney general Vernon

Thomson issued an opinion that public-sector bargaining was likely un-constitutional by restricting the discretion of legislative bodies regarding governmental functions. The WCCME introduced follow-up bills to 462-S introduced in the next three legislative sessions, and none of them gained any traction.

Unions amped up their electoral efforts in the 1954 governor's race where Democrat William Proxmire received a surprising 49 percent of the vote in a close loss. More than half of his funding came from labor unions. Republicans pushed back by passing the Caitlin Act in 1955. The bill banned political contributions by labor unions and was one of many nearly identical bills introduced across the Midwest that year—similar bills did not pass in Ohio and Michigan. It was supported by local and regional business interests, including Harry Bradley of the Allen-Bradley Company in Milwaukee.[20]

The ambiguous legal position of public employees was brought into focus when Milwaukee city dock workers got ensnarled in the Kohler strike in 1955. The Kohler Company was owned by the governor's relatives, though he had long since divested from it. The governor drew the ire of his cousin Herb Kohler, the company's president, when he appointed a fact-finding committee to investigate violence surrounding the strike. The company made a fortune in bathroom fixtures and was what historian Nelson Lichtenstein describes as one of many militant, often family-owned firms of the 1950s who were "quite unwilling to sign onto the Treaty of Detroit," and remained intransigent in their dealings with unions. The company had fought off union organizing attempts since the 1890s. After the UAW made inroads in 1952 and negotiated a one-year contract in 1953, the company refused to bargain and braced for a strike. Herb Kohler and his chief negotiator Lyman Conger kept the plants running. The strike was ugly and drawn out with plenty of violence on both sides. Exploits from the Kohler strike figured prominently in the McClellan Committee hearings later in the decade. But Herb Kohler's reputation got a boost in the business community as a result. He hit the chamber of commerce luncheon circuit at the end of the decade. Billed as a courageous individual who stood up to Big Labor, he used this forum to promote right-to-work legislation.[21]

Back in Milwaukee, city dock workers refused to unload a ship that was bound for a struck Kohler plant. They were AFSCME members and the company charged that they had engaged in a secondary boycott, which was prohibited under the Taft-Hartley Act. But in 1956 the NLRB ruled that as public employees they were exempt from the secondary boycott prohibitions in Taft-Hartley since they were not covered by the law. The legal gray area benefitting labor infuriated Kohler and the state's business community. The Wisconsin Chamber of Commerce called on the Legislative Council's Interim Committee on Labor Relations to recommend state legislation outlawing all forms of public-sector unionism. Chamber official Joseph Fagin argued that the NLRB decision had left the public "unprotected from big union-affiliated governmental labor organizations," and that "public employees are working for and should owe their loyalties to all of the people and not simply the big merged AFL-CIO" (though the state federations had yet to merge). Lawton responded that "[Public] employees don't always agree with conclusions or programs of members of the state Chamber, but we would never consider supporting legislation that would deny to businessmen the right to form an organization to promote business or for their mutual aid or protection." The Legislative Council's eventual report following the Kohler incident was mixed. It did not support an outright ban, as called for by the Chamber, but it offered no support for an affirmative state law either, instead leaving discretion to municipalities.[22]

While Fagin and the Chamber of Commerce were fearful of Big Labor coming to the public sector, WCCME remained something of an oddity within the state labor movement. WSFL president George Haberman had little interest in the WCCME or their ties to the new Democrats, whom he saw as brash and "too intellectual." He preferred to socialize with Republicans. More important, neither federation saw public-sector bargaining as a legislative priority to that point. The Kohler incident and the Chamber's response began to change this. The WSFL quickly passed a resolution in support of public-sector unionism and against the Chamber's attack as did Charles Schultz and the State Industrial Union Council. The postmerger Wisconsin AFL-CIO was publicly supportive of the WCCME and public-sector collective bargaining rights going forward.[23]

It was as the WCCME found some backing from the private-sector labor movement that Wisconsin Democrats made one of their first major breakthroughs. Republican divisions and their apparent overreach on labor raised the prospects for both Democrats and public-sector bargaining legislation at the end of the decade. The fissure between business leaders anxious to curb labor and more cautious political operatives proved disastrous in Ohio in 1958. In Wisconsin, the Chamber of Commerce had long pushed for right-to-work and other restrictions on unions and had had some success with the passage of the Caitlin Act in 1955. Privately business leaders pointed to the Caitlin Act as proof that you could target unions without electoral fallout, but few politicians were willing to bite. This anti-labor stance began to get more traction as the party grew cool to the "modern Republicanism" of Eisenhower and Walter Kohler. In the 1957 special election after Senator Joseph McCarthy's death, three-time gubernatorial candidate William Proxmire faced his nemesis in former governor Kohler. Kohler had survived a close, hard-fought primary in which he prided himself as the moderate choice. While Proxmire had developed name recognition from his campaigns over the decade, most attribute his surprising victory to the increasing dissension within the Republican Party. After the primary, many disaffected McCarthyites were still unwilling to support Kohler and stayed home. Proxmire won by more than 100,000 votes.[24]

The fallout from Kohler's loss exacerbated tensions within the party. At the state GOP convention in May 1958, party leaders tried to stress unity. Kohler and his primary opponent from 1957 both endorsed State Supreme Court Justice Roland Steinle to run against Proxmire in the general election. But when Kohler spoke, he was met with a spattering of boos.[25] Meanwhile, Republican delegates voted to introduce legislation for a state-wide referendum on right-to-work. The impetus came from Republicans in Madison and Milwaukee. The measure called for a Republican legislature to draft a bill and put it to the voters the first Tuesday in April 1959. By the end of the summer, two statewide right-to-work groups had formed.[26]

One consequence of this rightward move is that state Republicans more clearly resembled the reactionaries that unions campaigned against. When AFSCME president Arnold Zander claimed that the opponents of public-sector unions were the same people who opposed social security or had once fought restrictions on child labor, he now had two visible conservative activists to single out. The growing rift in the Republican Party also occurred as WCCME had clearly found a home within the rebuilt Democratic Party. Wisconsin Democrats included public-sector bargaining rights in their platform in 1958.

Republican governor Vernon Thomson did not want to run on right-to-work and did not support it publicly. Yet both he and Roland Steinle saw value in running against Walter Reuther and labor as a phantom candidate. Steinle repeatedly warned voters of the danger "presented by the labor bosses who are out to rule America." Thomson singled out his Democratic opponent Gaylord Nelson as being run by union "ringleaders" in Madison. Whereas John Lawton served on the Governor's Retirement Study Commission under

Kohler, Thomson declined to reappoint him. After ten years in the State Senate, most around Nelson thought this would be one of many runs to gain name recognition. But with strong labor support, Nelson beat Thomson by nearly 90,000 votes. Proxmire won the Senate race and, importantly for Lawton and the WCCME, Democrats gained a 55–45 majority in the State Assembly while Republicans maintained control of the Senate with a 20–13 majority.[27]

With a majority in the Assembly and a powerful ally in Governor Nelson, the WCCME needed to make their bill amenable to Republicans in the Senate. This time they excluded police from the outset. The companion bills introduced in February 1959 provided rights for municipal employees to form and join unions and to engage in "conference and negotiations" over wages, hours, and working conditions. Again the words "collective bargaining" did not appear. The public hearings over the bill were well-attended. Representatives from The Wisconsin League of Municipalities testified against the bill, warning of the threat to Home Rule posed by the Wisconsin Employment Relations Board (WERB). The *Wisconsin State Journal* editorialized against the specter of hospital workers and other necessary services going on strike as they had in New York City. But this time the momentum was clearly in the other direction. A majority of those testifying did so in favor of the bill. The competing claims on public employees had not changed much over the decade. Opponents emphasized the threat to state sovereignty and lambasted what they saw as a union takeover of government. The WCCME continued to argue that there were no sound reasons to deny public employees the basic associational rights held by everyone else—a theme they had brought before the legislature for several years now. In addition, Lawton testified to the retaliation and firings that union supporters regularly encountered.[28]

To increase the odds of passage, the WCCME made early compromises, agreeing to unfair labor practices on the part of unions and rights for employees to refrain from union activities. The Assembly passed this version 67–23, with all dissenting votes coming from Republicans. The Senate proved more difficult. Kirby Hendee, a Republican from Milwaukee, worked against the bill and sought more restrictive labor legislation with harsh penalties for public employees who struck. The Senate eventually passed an amendment further limiting the powers of the WERB, but it rejected another amendment exempting city and village employees from the bill. It also rejected Hendee's substitute amendment to outlaw public-sector strikes. The compromise bill with a weakened WERB split Republicans evenly, and all Democrats voted in favor. The Senate passed the bill 23–10 on July 23, and the Assembly did so the next day on a voice vote.[29]

Governor Nelson, the longtime friend and colleague of WCCME General Counsel John Lawton, signed the bill on September 23. The *City & County Union News* championed the public employee "Bill of Rights" as opening an enlightened era. WCCME executive director Robert Oberbeck reflected on the legislative accomplishment nearly a decade in the making:

> We may walk with our heads in the air, and with firm resolve that the Legislature of the state of Wisconsin has recognized that public employees are no longer second-class citizens, but first class citizens entitled to the same rights and protection of those rights as any other taxpayer in the state.[30]

The bill was limited. It was only a page long. There was no method to resolve an impasse and no explicit mandate for employers to bargain with workers and their representatives. These issues were hashed out in the coming years. Phillip "Buzz" Kuehn, the Republican candidate for governor in 1960, had advised Steinle in 1958 and embraced his strong anti-labor stance. He made his opposition to the new law and public-sector bargaining in general a campaign issue. Nelson's defeat of Kuehn that year seemingly validated the WCCME. A bill giving some teeth to 309-A passed the legislature and was signed into law by Nelson in January 1962. It gave the WERB authority to hold union elections and to mediate disputes if requested by both parties, it outlined Unfair Labor Practices, and it called for written contracts. Lawton saw this as the Magna Carta for municipal employees. Nelson was elected to the U.S. Senate in 1962 and went on to make his name on environmental issues, founding Earth Day in 1970. Lawton continued his practice and advocacy for public employees for the next two decades.[31]

AFSCME had arrived as a potent political organization in Wisconsin and its ties with an ascendant state Democratic Party would grow stronger over the next decade. By 1962, it was the fifth largest union in the state behind the Teamsters, Steelworkers, Machinists, and the UAW. In 1965, state employees were granted limited bargaining rights, while legislation in the early 1970s provided a mechanism for union-negotiated fair-share agreements that required employees covered by the collective bargaining contract to pay dues or a bargaining fee for the duration of the contract. Teachers, while slower to take advantage of the law and pursue collective bargaining, had become much more active and militant by the 1970s.[32]

Political Opportunities in the Wisconsin Case

The Wisconsin case did not involve a wide-ranging coalition. There was no sustained protest to pressure political officials. What is more, there was little support from the national labor movement, or even much interest from the state federations for most of the decade. Instead, the WCCME slowly cultivated political allies. Their consistent, and mostly quiet, legislative work paid off with the rise of the Wisconsin Democratic Party and the splintering of conservative opposition at the end of the decade. Lawton summed it up more succinctly in retrospect, "when the real enthusiasm was developing [for collective bargaining rights], Republicans had really shot their wad around here." Public-sector union activists succeeded when they did because of political opportunities.[33]

The insider route taken by public-sector union activists in Wisconsin was predicated on their strong ties to new Democrats. Like elsewhere, Wisconsin unions and the AFL-CIO's COPE contributed heavily to statewide Democratic candidates in the 1950s, and union volunteers provided additional resources in canvassing and get-out-the-vote drives. The Caitlin Act was passed in 1955 in response to union-backed Democratic gubernatorial candidate William Proxmire exceeding expectations in a narrow loss to Walter Kohler Jr. Yet union–party ties went beyond funding. Union activists played critical roles in the rebuilding of the Wisconsin Democratic Party during the decade. While the WSFL remained indifferent to New Democrats, individual unions, including AFSCME, worked hand in hand with them. Gaylord Nelson began his career working with AFSCME affiliate WCCME and its General Counsel John Lawton. Democrats included public-sector bargaining rights on their platform in 1958, and all Democrats voted in favor of the companion bargaining bills during the 1959 legislative session. Rather than outsiders trying to break in, union activists were critical from the outset.

Part of the WCCME's success was due to increasing dissension within the state Republican Party, where moderate and right-leaning factions had public splits over candidate selection, communism, and especially right-to-work. The Chamber of Commerce had long sought restrictions on unions as had some of the more activist employers. But these efforts were not championed by Walter Kohler Jr. and the Republican establishment for most of the decade. By 1957, however, more were willing to jump on board. The rightward direction of party leaders, inspired by the more strident anti-union approach by business leaders in the region, cost statewide candidates in the 1958 election. While Republicans still controlled the state Senate, they split evenly on the critical vote on public-sector bargaining rights, mostly mirroring the divisions within the party. Republicans voting against the measure tended to be business owners from conservative counties where Nelson fared worse.[34]

In this context of strong labor–Democratic ties and fissures among the opposition, the framing of union rights and the scope of the labor coalition pushing for them remained fairly narrow. Public-sector bargaining rights were characterized as an incremental change to labor regulation, one that provided public-sector workers the same associational rights accorded to anybody else, inside or outside of the labor movement. Active supporters did not extend far beyond WCCME and Democratic Party circles. If the campaign lacked the fanfare of Ohio, it shared the downplaying of union rights for their own sake. The merits of unionism or labor rights and economic fairness rarely figured into the proponents' arguments. This did not stop the Chamber of Commerce from warning the legislature and the public of the dangers of unionism and Big Labor coming to government. When public workers were ensnarled in the Kohler conflict, the ambiguity of public-sector bargaining rights was given a bigger public hearing. For most of the decade, however, the push for union rights was carried out within the confines of the legislature. This was the case both during the doldrums of the late 1940s and early 1950s as well as the more favorable climate at the end of the decade.

Public-sector workers in Wisconsin had some advantages that perhaps made their early organizing and legislative successes more likely than workers in other states. They were growing in numbers and the state had a pioneering legacy on labor and social issues. In this view, the expansion of employment protections for public-sector workers was the logical next step. Industrial relations experts increasingly saw public-sector unionism as reasonable and appropriate even if they disagreed on its exact form. What is more, progressives and labor officials gave life to the idea in Wisconsin prior to the New Deal. Yet progressivism was in the rearview mirror by the 1950s. More important for this case were the consistent legislative work by politically skilled public-sector union advocates throughout the 1950s and the strong ties they developed with a rebuilt state Democratic Party. When the shifting political winds at the end of the decade provided an opening, the WCCME had the political allies to capitalize. This differs from Ohio, where the new Democratic legislature in 1959 had a more strained relationship with unions and failed to implement many of labor's key goals.

The Aftermath

The adoption of the Wisconsin model elsewhere was a much more public and often contentious process. In the midst of the campaign to pass 309-A through the Wisconsin legislature in 1959, *Business Week* ran an article dubbing AFSCME "the union of the future" due to the untapped organizing potential of public-sector workers. The events of the coming decade would prove them right in some respects. In 1962, President Kennedy issued an executive order granting limited bargaining rights to federal employees. By the end of the 1960s it appeared that the great civil rights upsurge had spilled over into public-sector organizing. Dramatic conflicts in Memphis in 1968 and Charleston in 1969 underscored the potential of a now militant, public-sector union movement. Public-sector labor rights could no longer fly under the radar. Sixteen states had passed legislation granting at least some associational rights to state and local employees by the late 1960s. The new spate of public-sector laws were influential, if incomplete. Large groups of employees were often excluded. And in the development of public-sector rights in the heavily unionized states of the Midwest the process was uneven—a point I take up in the next chapter.[35]

Conclusion

Wisconsin union advocates took an insider route to securing public-sector labor rights. This route was made possible by the consistent union and Democratic Party organizing throughout the 1950s, the ties they formed, and the political opportunities at the end of the decade afforded by the strong rightward push and overreach of business activists and

Republicans. The Wisconsin model of public-sector recognition was not always quick to catch on in the industrial Midwest. There the development of public-sector organizing and union recognition was highly uneven and incomplete. At the dawn of the 1960s then, unions in the Midwest were in a holding pattern. They appeared to stave off the worst of the business offensive, but they were slow in advancing any progressive case for labor rights.

6

A Holding Pattern in the Midwest

The concerted push for restrictions on unions in the late 1950s caught the labor movement off guard. When employers went all in to curb unions in 1958, business likewise found itself in unfamiliar territory. The aggressive push by business activists surprised many of their closest political allies, and employers struggled to maintain the anti-labor coalition. Employer over-reach on right-to-work had lasting consequences, providing an opening for a long-dormant progressive labor policy in public-sector bargaining rights in Wisconsin. Right-to-work activity slowed following the 1958 elections to the point that, by the early 1960s, state chambers of commerce and most Republicans in the region were hesitant to push it. Burned by elec-toral fallout, business advocates instead sought out less contentious means of curbing labor. Public-sector collective bargaining took off in the decade following the Wisconsin law, but it was driven by very different factors. By the end of the 1960s, public-sector organizing intersected with major civil rights campaigns. Here again, Midwestern labor movements proceeded in an uneven manner and struggled to navigate familiar challenges of movement unity and often disinterested political allies.

This chapter picks up the story after the fallout over right-to-work and the breakthrough in public-sector collective bargaining rights. I take up both policy issues at the end of the 1950s and show how they caught on in the Midwest and elsewhere, roughly following the period of public-sector col-lective bargaining expansion over the next two decades. I then turn to the experience of the other two large industrial states in the region, Michigan and Illinois. While there are some notable differences within the region, such as the impressive labor–liberal coalition in Michigan, it is marked mostly by the disorganization of labor and its allies. Armed with this information, I place the key findings from chapters 3–5 in comparative perspective. I show that while there was no magic bullet for union influence, unions succeeded when they cultivated a broad coalition or influential political allies and, im-portantly, when their opposition crumbled. This required the presence of

Heartland Blues. Marc Dixon, Oxford University Press (2020). © Oxford University Press.
DOI: 10.1093/oso/9780190917036.001.0001.

unusually resourceful local activists or a push from far-sighted national organizations to overcome otherwise weak statewide organization.

State Labor Policies Going Forward

The Slowdown on Right-to-Work

The big labor story in the Midwest in 1959 was the steel strike. It was the biggest strike in US history in terms of person-hours lost. More than 500,000 workers struck, and nearly every steel plant was shuttered for months. Steelworkers president David McDonald had warned in 1958 that right-to-work backers were trying to soften up the union in advance of contract negotiations the following year. But the failure of right-to-work and anti-union campaigning in the region did not prevent the industry from digging in their heels. The two sides settled only after the Supreme Court upheld an injunction on national security grounds. While the steelworkers prevailed in retaining certain work rules in the contract, it didn't feel like a victory. The union was on the defensive. Steel imports gained a foothold in the process. And employers did not back down in the aftermath. The next year, General Electric beat an electrical workers' strike in what many saw as the triumph of "Boulwarism," the hard-nosed bargaining strategy championed by its namesake and GE vice president Lemuel Boulware.[1]

Despite the hard bargaining, employers and their Republican allies were less inclined to return to the contentious politics of right-to-work. Gilbert Gall's research found that state right-to-work campaigns usually forced unions and state labor federations to develop more sophisticated political and education programs and to forge closer relations with Democrats going forward.[2] This was mostly true in the Midwest. Yet the slowdown on right-to-work had as much if not more to do with changes in employer strategy. Business leaders, who had jumped ahead of their political allies in the 1958 elections, sought to avoid the spotlight and backed away from right-to-work activity in industrial states after the election losses. At the same time, the National Right to Work Committee (NRTWC), regrouped under new leadership, embraced far-right politics and ultimately moved resources away from state legislative campaigns and toward litigation.

Labor also chipped away at the biggest victory by right-to-work forces in Indiana by challenging a loophole in the law. In a major blunder, the authors of the law did not include an explicit prohibition of nonmembers being charged some representation fee if not dues, or an "agency shop." The UAW contested GM's refusal to bargain over the agency shop in Indiana with the National Labor Relations Board (NLRB) in early 1961. The NLRB first dismissed the union's claim but agreed to reconsider the case after the board was reshuffled with President Kennedy's appointees. This time the NLRB sided with the union, acknowledging that in the absence of a specific prohibition, nonmembers could be charged a representation fee. It still took time for unions and Democrats to get on the same page to repeal the Indiana law, though they came together at the right moment. The nationwide Democratic landslide in 1964 gave the party control over government for the first time since the 1930s. A more unified labor movement worked with Democrats and successfully repealed right-to-work in March 1965, this time without much fanfare.[3]

The national labor movement's ambitions were bigger than the Indiana repeal. In the initial afterglow of the 1958 contests, the AFL-CIO sought to repeal section 14(b) of the Taft-Hartley Act, which permits states to pass and enforce right-to-work laws, thereby eliminating the state-by-state strategy in one swoop. Congress showed no interest. Instead, the culmination of the McClellan Committee resulted in the Landrum-Griffin Act of 1959, which sought to rein in financial malfeasance by unions. With no prospects in Congress, the AFL-CIO's executive council laid out their state-by-state alternative. The aggressive plan, hatched in the spring of 1959, called for the AFL-CIO to help state labor movements repeal existing right-to-work laws across a range of contexts, including a new ballot initiative in Kansas and renewed legislative efforts in Indiana and Utah and even in long-forgotten southern states like North Carolina. Little of this came to fruition. Despite the ambitious plans, Indiana in 1965 was the only repeal effort to make it to a vote. Renewed efforts to repeal 14(b) during the Johnson administration were also unsuccessful.[4]

GE's Lemuel Boulware was one of the most prominent business voices for right-to-work in the late 1950s. In 1958, he gave talks across the country on the urgent need for businessmen to take a stand in politics. After the elections, he called instead for caution. His postmortem on right-to-work from November 1958 stated that businessmen must exert better "leadership in researching public opinions . . . Exert appropriate influence in the *timing* of future campaigns—in picking states where there is at least a fair chance of victory in a given year." More generally, he wanted business to recede from the face of these campaigns. Any new efforts, Boulware suggested, should come from "broadly-based organizations, with members representing the clergy, farm groups, the professions, *and union members*, as well as businessmen" (emphasis in original). This was needed to overcome "the potent opposition charge that RTW campaigns are 'big-business' projects." NAM public affairs director Carl Biemiller agreed, suggesting business should focus on "practical politics at the grass roots," not big controversial campaigns like right-to-work.[5]

State business federations in the Midwest mostly agreed and stayed clear of the issue in 1959. John Tharp, labor relations director for the Illinois Chamber of Commerce, said it was no longer a "hot issue." Instead, his organization pushed Landrum-Griffin-style reforms targeting union corruption and "racket picketing." The latter reforms putatively concerned unions' use of picketing to extort businesses, though in practice the laws were often used to reel in picketing used during union organizing drives. Chamber of Commerce leaders in Ohio also pushed for Landrum-Griffin-style reforms after their landslide loss on right-to-work. Republicans who were willing to align with business activists on an aggressive anti-labor strategy likewise broke off. A Republican official in Michigan later conveyed to political scientist David Greenstone, "In 1958 our campaign was based on hanging [UAW president] Walter Reuther, [UAW secretary-treasurer Emil] Mazey, and [Michigan AFL-CIO president Gus] Scholle. In 1960, the issue was dead—it's a good sign."[6]

The NRTWC had a more optimistic take considering the election losses. Reed Larson, director of the successful Kansas initiative, became executive vice president of the organization and worked to revive the issue, particularly in the Midwest. Unlike Boulware, Larson suggested right-to-work could win at the polls only when "business leaders come out from behind the cloak of anonymity afforded by business organizations to let it be known that they, as individuals, believe in freedom from compulsory unionism." He and his assistants met with interested business owners in Pennsylvania, Illinois, and Michigan. According to a Group Research report, NRTWC membership and revenues spiked in the early 1960s. But this appears to have been driven by the enthusiasm of the far right rather than collaboration with mainstream state employer associations like the chamber of commerce. In an interview with the *Wall Street Journal*, Larson attributed the growth of the NRTWC to the "wave of conservative feeling that Sen[*sic*] Goldwater spoke of, not only in the colleges but all through the country," noting that his organization emphasized a similar brand of "militant patriotism."[7]

Table 6.1 shows all right-to-work votes in the two decades following the 1958 landslide. Much of the activity involved strengthening existing right-to-work laws or bringing new ones to a vote in areas where unions were weak. Activity stalled in the large industrial states. Even before 1958, there was tension between state business associations, employers, and the national right-to-work movement. While Indiana had a model campaign in this respect, employers struggled with many of the same coordination problems that unions grappled with. These difficulties became more pronounced after the elections when fewer politicians and business federations were willing to push the issue. The U.S. Chamber of Commerce formed a committee on voluntary unionism in 1961, but it struggled to recapture the momentum of the late 1950s. The 1964 Democratic landslide and the subsequent repeal of right-to-work in Indiana in 1965 further dimmed their prospects. While right-to-work was introduced in Indiana in nearly every legislative session following the repeal, it did not garner support from significant numbers of Republicans for the next three decades. The situation was similar across the region. The only new votes on right-to-work in the 1960s, in addition to the repeal in Indiana, were in Oklahoma and Wyoming. The Kansas legislature passed enabling

Table 6.1 State Action on Right-to-Work, 1958–1978

State	Year	Action
Mississippi	1960	Constitutional amendment passed (strengthening 1954 statute)
Wyoming	1963	Statute passed
Oklahoma	1964	Statute failed
Indiana	1965	Repeal passed
Kansas	1969	Enabling legislation for 1958 constitutional amendment vetoed
Kansas	1975	Enabling legislation for 1958 constitutional amendment passed
Arkansas	1976	Repeal failed
Louisiana	1976	Statute passed
New Mexico	1977	Statute failed
Missouri	1978	Statute failed

Sources: Gall (1988); Jacobs and Dixon (2006).

legislation with harsher civil penalties for their existing constitutional amendment, but Democratic governor Robert Docking vetoed the bill.[8]

Amid the slowdown in state right-to-work campaigns and the limited possibility of a national right-to-work law, the NRTWC decided to shift resources toward litigation that challenged the constitutionality of union security. Staff dedicated to litigation doubled over the 1960s, culminating in the formation of the National Right to Work Legal Defense Foundation. Larson and the foundation modeled their efforts on the NAACP's Legal Defense Fund. They sought to develop a pro-worker, pro-civil-rights public image. Several of their key cases involved black plaintiffs.[9] By the late 1960s, they turned their attention to the increasingly organized and militant public-sector workers movement. They sued on behalf of dissident union members in the aftermath of a teachers' strike in Detroit. In the 1970s, their work intersected with anti-labor strategist and law professor Sylvester Petro. Petro, whose work underpinned more recent legal setbacks to public-sector unions, most notably the Supreme Court's 2018 decision in the *Janus v. AFSCME* case, worked with Larson and other conservative activists against the specter of a national public-sector law.[10]

The fallout after the 1958 elections prompted different responses from right-to-work advocates. As state Republican Parties backed away from the issue in the Midwest, so too did their traditional allies in mainstream employer associations like the NAM and the U.S. Chamber of Commerce. The NRTWC worked to revive the issue under new leadership but soon shifted resources toward what they saw as a more fruitful litigation strategy. And while the AFL-CIO hatched an ambitious state-by-state strategy for repeal, they made little headway outside of Indiana. Collectively, this led to a slowdown in right-to-work activity on both sides.

The Takeoff in Public-Sector Collective Bargaining

The Wisconsin law emerged out of the fallout over right-to-work and dissension among Republicans in the region. The takeoff of public-sector legislation following Wisconsin was a much more public and contentious process. In 1962, President Kennedy issued an executive order granting collective bargaining rights to federal employees. By the end of the decade, it appeared that the great civil rights upsurge had spilled over into public-sector organizing. Dramatic conflicts in Memphis, Tennessee, in 1968 and Charleston,

South Carolina, in 1969 underscored the potential of a now-militant public-sector union movement. And in 1970, postal workers engaged in a highly disruptive wildcat strike that brought about legislation enabling them to collectively bargain.[11]

By the peak of public-sector union activism in the mid-1970s, twenty states had passed affirmative bargaining laws for state employees, eight held outright bans on union organization, and the rest had no statute or had weaker "meet and confer" provisions that technically allowed for unions to exist but did not require public employers to actually bargain with them. The situation for police, teachers, and municipal workers was similar. States that passed enabling laws tended to be more liberal and urbanized. The bans on collective bargaining predictably were in states without much union presence, including Texas, Virginia, and much of the Deep South, though the industrial Midwest also lagged behind, as I will show.[12]

The bans in the South meant that even the most promising crossovers between labor and civil rights activism were slowed by hard political realities. A year after the sanitation strike and protest campaign in Memphis, where Martin Luther King Jr. was assassinated, the Southern Christian Leadership Conference (SCLC) partnered with hospital union affiliate Local 1199 of the Retail, Wholesale and Department Store Union in a strike at the Medical College of South Carolina in Charleston. It was an epic one-hundred-day event led by an almost entirely black and female workforce. Protests headlined by national civil rights leaders, including Coretta Scott King and Andrew Young, rocked the quiet city. All prominent liberals worth their name backed the workers. Yet at the end of the day, administrators refused to budge on union recognition. South Carolina governor Robert McNair told hospital trustees to hold firm, that the union and SCLC were going to "die hard" and "probably look for a better atmosphere somewhere outside of South Carolina to continue the fight." To this day, the state does not authorize public-sector collective bargaining.[13]

Figure 6.1 plots the average public-sector bargaining rights for the industrial Midwest in comparison to regions with high (Northeast) and low (South) bargaining rights from 1955 to 1985, covering the period of the expansion of rights. The score aggregates the rights of five different employee groups—state, police, fire, teachers, and local employees—by region. For each group, the score ranges from no rights (0) to the opportunity to meet and confer with employers but no mandate to bargain (1) to collective bargaining rights with at least some mandate to bargain (2). A score of 10

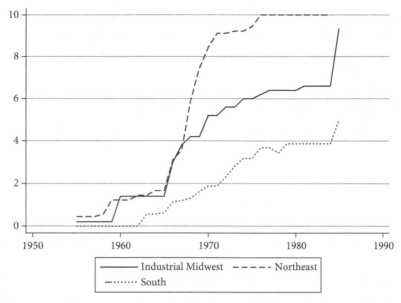

Figure 6.1 Public-Sector Bargaining Rights across the Industrial Midwest, Northeast, and South

Note: Y axis sums collective bargaining rights for state workers, police, fire, teachers, and local employees (0 = no rights for any group; 10 = full rights with a mandate bargain for all groups).
Source: Valletta and Freeman (1988).

indicates that all five groups have bargaining rights and employers have a mandate to bargain; a score of 0 indicates that none of them do.

While laws were often incomplete, had no mandate to bargain, or excluded certain groups, there was a surge in collective bargaining rights from the mid-1960s through the 1970s. As Figure 6.1 and Table 6.2 show, in the heavily unionized states of the Midwest, the process was uneven and often delayed, placing the region somewhere in between the northeast and the south in the development of public-sector bargaining rights.

Michigan passed a comprehensive bill following the Democratic landslide in the 1964 elections and the reapportionment of the state legislature providing greater urban representation. Though malapportionment often worked against labor movements rooted in urban areas, the Midwest, with the exception of Ohio, ranked in the top third in terms of the most representative states in the 1950s.[14] In Ohio, the main public-sector law on the books for decades was the Ferguson Act of 1947, which banned public employee strikes and called for strikers to be fired. Unions had some momentum

Table 6.2 Adoption of Public-Sector Bargaining
Rights in the Industrial Midwest

	Local	State
Illinois[1]	1984	1973
Indiana[2]	1973	1989
Ohio	1983	1983
Michigan	1965	1976
Wisconsin	1959	1965

[1] State employees initially granted rights by executive order.
[2] 1973 law for teachers only; 1989 was by executive order.
Source: Valletta and Freeman (1988).

following the big right-to-work vote in 1958. With Democratic control of
both houses, union supporters made inroads with the passage of Senate Bill
209, which allowed for voluntary deduction of union dues but did not authorize collective bargaining. While public-sector union organizing, bargaining, and, increasingly, striking picked up in the late 1960s and 1970s, it
was not until the election of labor-friendly Democrat Dick Celeste as governor in the depths of the recession in 1982 that union supporters were able
to enact a comprehensive public-sector bargaining bill. The laggard status of
Ohio was due partly to the demands of the state AFL-CIO for a strong statute
or none at all but mostly due to the intransigence of popular Republican governor Jim Rhodes. Illinois likewise did not pass comprehensive legislation
until the 1980s because of opposition from the building trades unions and
the Chicago Democratic machine. As I describe later, the prospect of collective bargaining legislation threatened existing handshake relationships and
the jurisdiction of building trades unions.[15]

In Indiana, various bargaining bills were introduced in the 1960s and 1970s
and unions failed to coalesce behind any one of them. Facing a series of teacher
strikes in the early 1970s, the Republican-dominated legislature surprisingly
passed a collective bargaining bill for teachers in 1973, creating the Indiana
Education Employment Relations Board. Many other public employees only
gained bargaining rights much later through the executive order of Democratic
governor Evan Bayh in 1989—a directive that was rescinded in 2006 by
Republican governor Mitch Daniels.[16] Even in Wisconsin, where labor–
Democratic ties were strengthened through a series of collective bargaining

bills, the relationship between the two was tested. Governor Patrick Lucey, who was central to building the Democratic Party in the 1950s, had little love for public-sector unions by the mid-1970s. He took a hard line in bargaining. When state employees went on strike in 1977, he and his immediate successor, Democrat Martin Schreiber, sought to discipline strikers against the tenets of the amnesty clause agreed upon by the union and the state. They were supported in this effort by Democratic attorney general Bronson La Follette.[17]

By the early 1970s, AFSCME president Jerry Wurf and other public-sector activists sought to address the "shameful hodgepodge" of piecemeal state and local policies with a national law guaranteeing all public-sector workers collective bargaining rights. Its prospects faltered as a mounting financial crisis and unpopular public-sector strikes sparked a significant conservative backlash. As historian Joseph McCartin describes, one unanticipated consequence of the push for far-reaching public-sector labor rights was the galvanizing of conservative activists around public finances and taxes. Public-sector unions, which sneaked in under the radar in Wisconsin in 1959, were now a favored target of the right—something that has only increased since.[18]

Other Industrial States

If there was a case for labor influence being seamless from the bargaining table to the political arena and where unions made a strong case for labor rights, it was in Michigan, where the UAW backed a strong liberal–labor coalition.[19] Here political opportunities and organization were both favorable for labor. Illinois, by contrast, was marked by divisions within the labor movement and ambivalence on the part of Democratic allies. Though, as we shall see, the Michigan labor movement faced a host of challenges familiar to its neighbors.

Michigan

Michigan differed from its Midwestern peers in a few respects. David Greenstone described it as the "most ambitious example of labor political action of the time."[20] It started with the unique position of the UAW and the auto industry. The UAW dominated the Michigan labor movement such that other unions just did not have the resources to compete. The UAW also provided a home base for liberals outside of the labor movement by hiring them as researchers and other staff. The combination of an ideologically committed large union with no peers in the state, a weak Democratic Party, and legal restrictions on patronage allowed the UAW to effectively take over the state Democratic Party in the late 1940s. The linking of Democrats as the pro-labor party in the public imagination probably came a decade earlier when then governor Frank Murphy refused to bring in the National Guard to break up the Flint sit-down strike in the winter of 1936–1937.[21]

Labor's imprint on Democratic politics in Michigan cannot be understated. A study of the 1956 presidential election found that 39 percent of Democratic voters in Wayne County were affiliated with CIO unions, most with the UAW. And the UAW's influence did not end there. As a business leader in Detroit put it, "[We've] found it increasingly hard to be anti-UAW and still be a local booster."[22] Union towns existed across the Midwest, of course, but the place of the UAW—and, by extension, the labor movement in the social and political fabric of Detroit (and, to a lesser degree, the state)—was in many ways exceptional.

The state AFL CIO, which formed at the beginning of 1958, reflected the liberal vision of the UAW. It was strongly pro–civil rights and supported an expansive social welfare system. It had an extensive education department. It provided members with the latest right-to-work materials and films generated by the national AFL-CIO. It even subsidized copies of C. Wright Mills's *The Power Elite* for union members. There was still pushback from the building trades unions. Some joined the Wayne County AFL-CIO but initially refused to affiliate with the state body, headed by the liberal Gus Scholle. Still, conflict within the labor movement was comparatively muted, mostly because the UAW was so dominant.[23]

During this time, the state GOP was just as strongly identified with the auto industry. The transfer of union–employer dynamics from the bargaining table to the political realm was more pronounced there than anywhere before or after. George Romney, former president of American Motors Corporation, served as a Republican governor in the 1960s. Ford and General Motors officials dominated different county delegations. And they all sought a conservative vision of government.[24]

From the late 1940s through the 1950s, Republicans maintained control of the state legislature while the liberal–labor coalition succeeded in electing Democrat G. Mennen "Soapy" Williams to a record six terms as governor as well as sending a liberal congressional delegation to Capitol Hill. The well-off liberals in the labor coalition, like Williams and congressman Neil Staebler from Ann Arbor, were described by their opponents as "millionaires who take orders from Walter Reuther." At times, this appeared to be the case. Williams initially refused to extradite a UAW organizer who had fled Wisconsin after a violent altercation with a scab during the Kohler strike. But he changed his tune after Walter Reuther testified before the McClellan Committee that the organizer should stand trial in Wisconsin. More often, though, the highly popular Williams kept unions from being the face of the party.[25]

Even in this favorable context, unions faced some familiar problems. In 1960, Carl Stellato, president of UAW Local 600, representing the giant Ford River Rouge Complex, asked the Wayne County AFL-CIO *not* to endorse him in the Democratic primary, as many had attributed his prior defeats to his union office. Union-backed candidates also fared poorly in nonpartisan mayoral elections where unions were visible and the Democratic Party was not.[26]

By the end of the 1950s, the NRTWC had made some inroads in the state. It supported organizations across the Midwest and began taking out advertisements in Michigan newspapers in the fall of 1957. The ads typically highlighted the plight of disenchanted union members, most of them UAW members. Joe Walsh, the UAW's assistant public relations director, warned union officials at the time that the NRTWC could "visit serious harm" on the union movement in Michigan. Following its lead, the state GOP put right-to-work in the labor plank in their election-year platform in 1958. The elections that year slowed the momentum of right-to-work everywhere. NRTWC efforts in the early 1960s to revive the issue in Michigan never really took off. In 1962, NRTWC state activities director Charles Bailey spoke to the Genesee County Conservative Club in Flint. The group planned a local right-to-work committee, but the state GOP had mostly moved on.[27]

Unions' biggest accomplishments in the legislature during the 1950s were the forestalling of anti-labor initiatives. The threat of right-to-work was lessened in Michigan because Williams was a popular governor and assured unions he would veto anything that came across his desk. The state AFL-CIO was also much more active and cohesive in Michigan than elsewhere. In a letter to Walter Reuther in June 1958, Michigan AFL-CIO president Gus Scholle summed up a key problem most state labor movements faced on right-to-work. With all the focus on "free riders," Scholle wrote, "we cannot but wonder why the principle of 'union' and 'closed' shop is not applied in the relationship between AFL-CIO chartered unions and the subordinate state and local central bodies. These bodies are responsible for the united action of unions in the political and legislative fields, but they are continually hampered by the activities or lack of activity on the part of 'free riding' unions." Michigan differed in this respect, according to Scholle. "A large part of the credit for the ability of the [Michigan] central labor body to perform this valuable service, is that the attitude of the international union whose membership constitutes the majority of the union membership in the state has been cooperative." The position of the UAW meant that not only were there resources available for the state federation but that most everyone was on the same page. For Scholle, this allowed the Michigan labor movement to fight back against the "forces of reaction even though these forces were led by the mighty 'big three' of the automobile industry."[28]

By the 1960s, the liberal–labor coalition moved from helping to forestall anti-labor initiatives to advancing public-sector labor rights. Like many other states, Michigan had adopted restrictive public-sector legislation during the conservative wave of 1947. The Hutchinson Act called for the firing of public-sector strikers and did not authorize collective bargaining. The Michigan Public Employment Relations Act of 1965 came a year after reapportionment and the anti-Goldwater liberal landslide. The results were swift. Not much had changed between the 1940s, when a handful of municipalities had informal agreements with public-sector unions, and the early 1960s. In the five years after the law's passage, more than 70 percent of towns with populations of 4,000 and over had collective bargaining agreements. Some 1,500 labor agreements were signed within the first two years the act was in force. This was led by AFSCME affiliates, though private-sector unions got into the act as well, including the Teamsters, who organized school bus drivers. By the late 1960s, militant teachers had become the face of the public-sector labor movement.[29]

Illinois

Like the other states considered here, Illinois boasted a large labor movement and industrial workforce, particularly in steel and auto. Labor organization and its influence in politics was uneven, putting it closer to the three focal states than to Michigan. Patronage in state and local politics limited the industrial unions' influence while boosting the clout of the building trades unions in Chicago. Downstate Democrats sometimes collaborated with Republicans just out of spite for the Chicago machine. Mostly this led to a lack of activity. While Illinois was a fairly competitive state, one 1950s study found that nearly three-quarters of all roll-call votes in the legislature were unanimous. Business and labor federations sometimes worked together on unemployment insurance prior to legislative activity. This "agreed-upon bill process" held for parts of the 1940s and early 1950s but less so in the following decades. During the postwar years, Illinois was marked by little labor legislation, pro or anti. Right-to-work was forestalled in the late 1950s when conservative advocates misread the political climate, while public-sector collective bargaining rights were delayed for decades due to opposition from the Chicago machine.[30]

For labor and for Democrats, everything began in Chicago. The Democratic machine headed by Mayor Richard J. Daley had significant support from labor and business leaders, as well as some of the seamier elements in the city. Nationally, many city machines fell off after the New Deal. Chicago's persisted well into the 1970s. It was only broken by Daley's death in 1976 and, finally, the election of the city's first African American mayor Harold Washington in 1983. Washington, who received significant support from AFSCME, opposed patronage as a relic that perpetuated racial inequality.[31]

In the mid-1950s, AFL unions outnumbered CIO unions by three to one. Although the state federations merged in late 1958, the powerful Chicago Federation of Labor (CFL) refused to do so until 1962. The building trades unions of the CFL were often successful in shaping local regulations that directly impacted their members' jobs, while social reform efforts by the CIO's industrial unions were largely shut out. CIO unions, mainly the UAW, made an unsuccessful attempt to challenge the Democratic machine in 1950. After that, the party was mostly indifferent to them. They welcomed the AFL-CIO's COPE and the big industrial unions for national elections, where union volunteers were typically more informed than local party workers. And the industrial unions were critical in some statewide elections, helping to elect prominent liberals like Adlai Stevenson to the governorship and senator Paul Douglas to the U.S. Senate. But Daley's machine kept them at arm's length. CFL leaders were much closer to Daley. William McFetridge from the Building Service Employees International Union and William Lee of the Teamsters both curried favor with the mayor. They and the CFL, which they dominated, stuck to the informal relationships that served them well and were often a key veto on progressive legislation, including public-sector bargaining.[32]

Anti-labor organization took off in Illinois in the late 1950s. The Illinois Right-to-Work Committee formed in the spring of 1957 following the Indiana victory and had close ties to the conservative Conference of American Small Business Organizations. Early on, however, it struggled to raise funds or garner support from key Republicans. Right-to-work was introduced in the Illinois House that spring and hurriedly brought before a judiciary committee hearing despite opposition from moderate Republican governor William Stratton. The effort was poorly coordinated. Given the potential veto from Stratton, few Republicans wanted to embrace it publicly, and the committee chair sent it back to a subcommittee where it idled. *Chicago Tribune* columnist George Tagge noted that rushing the bill by right-to-work supporters without much legwork did "no favor for the conservative cause."[33] Right-to-work supporters regrouped and briefly floated the idea of an amendment to the Illinois Constitution, which would require a public vote. Into October 1958, Illinois Manufacturers' Association executive vice president James Donnelly remained confident the legislature would adopt a right-to-work statute in the next session or two. But after the November election, neither his organization nor the state chamber of commerce actively pushed the issue.[34]

If right-to-work activists were out of step with state politics, labor had their own problems. Reuther and the AFL-CIO provided increased financial and strategic support to state affiliates as right-to-work heated up during the summer of 1958. The national strategy emphasized the larger issues at stake, including social security, and outreach to community groups so that right-to-work was not seen as solely a labor issue. None of this appeared to make it to Illinois. The Illinois AFL-CIO Executive Board reported their new strategy on right-to-work at the 1958 merger convention. Whereas prior union attempts to counter the appeal of the right-to-work, like "right-to-wreck" or "right-to-scab," mostly fell flat, the board touted the technical "compulsory open shop" as a new way forward. The new slogan did not stick. There was no mention of outreach to non-labor constituencies.[35]

The fallout over right-to-work did not lead to any breakthroughs on public-sector bargaining as it did in Wisconsin. The Illinois General Assembly passed an early public-sector collective bargaining bill in 1945, only to be vetoed by moderate Republican governor Dwight Green, otherwise a friend of labor. As AFSCME fully embraced collective bargaining in the 1960s, its affiliates in Illinois were hamstrung by resistance from their most likely ally in big-city Democrats. Chicago Democrats sought to maintain patronage arrangements and so did their key labor allies. The building trades unions of the CFL benefitted from handshake agreements with Daley on public projects and opposed any legal recognition of public-sector workers that would upend this or threaten their jurisdiction. This left small groups of downstate Democrats pushing for public-sector labor rights while the unlikely mix of Republicans and Chicago Democrats opposed them. Democratic governor Dan Walker, frustrated with the lack of legislative action, granted state employees collective bargaining rights by executive order in 1973. It would take another decade before a confluence of factors, most notably the decline of machine politics and backing by the CFL and Chicago Democrats along with increasingly organized teachers, helped bring about comprehensive public-sector legislation in Illinois.[36]

Taken together, Michigan and Illinois show both the possibility and common limits of labor political influence in the states. Michigan, with a single dominant and socially liberal union, parleyed strength at the bargaining table into an impressive liberal–labor coalition that forestalled anti-labor legislation in the 1950s and successfully backed progressive legislation in the 1960s. Illinois was marked by a divided labor movement and a Democratic Party that had little interest in the large industrial unions, save for big elections. While right-to-work advocates stumbled in the late 1950s, the union movement similarly failed to coalesce around public-sector collective bargaining rights for decades.

Revisiting the Campaigns

Table 6.3 plots the main factors and outcomes across the three labor rights campaigns and for Illinois and Michigan more generally.[37] Recall that the social movement explanations outlined at the beginning of the book suggest that movement influence in politics is fleeting because of the many moving parts necessary—that is, the right mix of political opportunities, movement and countermovement organizations, and competing insider and outsider strategies—for grassroots groups to make a difference. For each of the three sets of factors, I indicate in the table their basic character (e.g., whether political opportunities were strong or poor, organizations unified or divided, and the dominant political strategy insider or outsider) and how they played

Table 6.3 Main Factors and Outcomes for the Five Industrial States

	Anti-Labor/Mixed		Pro-Labor		
	Indiana	Illinois	Ohio	Wisconsin	Michigan
Political Opportunities					
Labor	**Poor:** Patronage party organization; industrial unions peripheral player in Democratic Party coalition	**Mixed:** Patronage party organization benefitted building trades but not industrial unions	**Poor:** Decentralized, Democratic patronage organization precluded strong role for labor statewice	**Strong:** WCCME and public-sector activists central in rebuilding Democratic Party	**Strong:** Well-organized labor-Democratic Party coalition headed by UAW
Countermovement	**Strong:** Both parties receptive to Chamber of Commerce; key Republicans back NRTWC	**Strong:** ties between business associations and Republican Party	**Poor:** Republican Party leaders disfavored RTW in election year; discord between party leaders and RTW campaign	**Poor:** Dissension on the right weakened employer influence within the Republican Party	**Strong:** Well-organized Republican Party with strong ties to automakers
Organization					
Labor	**Divided:** Divisions between building trades and industrial unions preclude joint action on RTW, spill over into public disputes	**Divided:** State federations late to merge due to objections of building trades	**Unified:** State federations late to merge, but UOLO successful in coordirating activity on RTW with assistance from AFL-CIO	**Mixed:** State federations late to merge; WCCME successful in coordinating campaign activity	**Unified:** Strong state AFL-CIO backed by single dominant union in UAW

(continued)

Table 6.3 *Continued*

	Anti-Labor/Mixed		Pro-Labor		
	Indiana	**Illinois**	**Ohio**	**Wisconsin**	**Michigan**
Countermovement	**Unified:** State Chamber of Commerce successfully recruited firms, workers, and politicians to support RTW campaign	**Divided:** State business associations and state RTW organization split on strategy	**Divided:** Some local Chamber of Commerce affiliates defect from RTW campaign; insular group of business leaders at the end	**Mixed:** Strong employer political organization; limited coordination with state RTW organizations	**Mixed:** Strong employer political organization backed by automakers; limited coordination with RTW activists
Strategy					
Labor	**Insider:** Worked within the legislature; AFL leaders disfavored coalitions	**Insider:** Building trades work with Democratic machine; little attempt to engage outside allies	**Outsider:** Successfully recruited religious and civil society partners to participate in RTW campaign	**Insider:** No attempt to engage outside allies; quiet legislative work with Democrats	**Insider & Outsider:** Liberal–labor coalition engages community partners beyond Democratic Party
Countermovement	**Insider & Outsider:** Combined lobbying with outreach to workers, businesses, and community organizations	**Insider:** Worked within the legislature	**Outsider:** Sought out business and community partners with little success	**Insider:** Worked within the legislature	**Insider:** Worked within the legislature

out for *both* labor and the business-led countermovements across the five industrial states. In general, unions succeeded when they forged a broad coalition and when they cultivated influential political allies. Both routes required a break from the routine of divided labor federations and disinterested politicians. And both benefitted from the employer opposition imploding.

Across the three campaigns, political opportunities for unions were mixed and driven by the organization and interest of both labor and the major parties in the states. The region leaned Republican in state politics, and some AFL state federations and big unions, like the Teamsters, endorsed Republican candidates. In patronage-oriented states, unions—particularly the industrial unions—were mostly peripheral players in the Democratic coalition. This diminished union influence and meant that the typical exchange relationships between unions and Democratic officeholders were not always smooth. It was a Democrat who introduced right-to-work in the Indiana House. Even after labor helped usher in a Democratic legislature in Ohio in 1958, the new Democratic governor remained aloof to unions' legislative goals and instead argued for restrictions on labor before the Ohio House Judiciary Committee. Unions fared better with issue-oriented parties, though this too was uneven. Individual unions, like AFSCME, helped rebuild the Democratic Party in Wisconsin, which paid off for public-sector collective bargaining rights, while the state AFL-CIO was much slower to embrace them or acknowledge the place of public-sector unions.

Effective organization or the lack thereof shaped the ability of unions to navigate more or less friendly political environments, seek out new allies, and push back against their opponents. This hinged first and foremost on union divisions, particularly animus between industrial and building trades unions, which reached dysfunctional levels in Indiana, where AFL leaders accused the UAW and the Steelworkers of sabotaging their efforts on right-to-work. This tension precluded coalition work or even a coordinated attempt to work with legislators. Ohio also had significant divisions, and the state labor federations were late to merge, yet union divisions were effectively muted during the campaign. Here, moving away from this disorganized state of affairs required a push from the outside in the form of support from the national labor movement and the hiring of a sophisticated public relations firm to plot out the campaign and actively recruit union members and community partners to participate. The external push and expertise, not surprisingly, tied back to Walter Reuther and the UAW. While the CIO and then the AFL-CIO had sought to cultivate community allies with varying degrees of success, this focus did not always make its way to state labor movements. In Wisconsin, as elsewhere, public-sector labor activists remained on the outside of the state labor movement for most of the decade. Their success in navigating a changing political environment there rested on an unusually resourceful network of local activists who directly shaped and participated in Democratic politics.

My emphasis on the negative effects of labor divisions is at odds with some research that finds benefits to conflict. For example, Judith Stepan-Norris and Caleb Southworth find that rival unionism led to increases in union density over the twentieth century. And, indeed, the CIO upsurge in the 1930s and 1940s forced AFL unions to organize and become more politically active. After these moments of insurgency, however, divisions complicate routine political tasks and diminish labor's one key advantage in the size of its membership.[38]

Increased support from the AFL-CIO in the late 1950s helped streamline and address the organizational deficits of state labor movements to an extent. The national federation pressured state AFL and CIO affiliates to merge and work together in the political field, though some powerful local affiliates and member unions still refused. The outward-looking strategy developed by the AFL-CIO on right-to-work made it to some states but not to others. More generally, state political contexts varied in significant enough ways to preclude a collective solution. The development and diffusion of best practices on labor campaigns still depended on the organization and receptiveness of state labor movements to pass them on. Moreover, none of this provided a quick solution to the mixed interest and availability of labor's likely allies, whether in politics or in the community.

Given these limitations, it is perhaps not surprising that unions mostly stuck to insider strategies to defend and advance labor rights, even when political allies were few. Unions in Ohio were forced to take an alternative path when the state chamber of commerce launched the ballot initiative for right-to-work. In this case, the labor movement built a far-reaching coalition. Community, and especially religious ties, provided a critical buffer from business claims of union corruption. The coalition also removed labor and union leaders from the face of right-to-work as they had been in Indiana. The coalition in Ohio thus contributed to a more compelling framing of labor rights, making right-to-work bigger than just a labor issue. Here, a more convincing argument on right-to-work meant having other—that is, non-labor—actors make the case for them. However, the idea that coalition partners could bring increased credibility or legitimacy was lost on most state labor movements, which had little time or interest for outreach. For example, AFL leaders in Indiana scoffed at the idea of the legislature putting right-to-work to a public vote, arguing that labor legislation only concerned union members.

The effectiveness of business-led countermovements in these conflicts can also be understood in terms of opportunity, organization, and strategy. Indeed, drawn to the same arenas, unions and employers often pursued similar competing strategies. With controversial issues like right-to-work, employers were forced to seek out new allies, including workers, for legitimacy. This worked to great effect in Indiana but proved more difficult elsewhere. Like labor, employers struggled with divisions and coordination problems. The big auto and steel firms stayed on the sidelines across the region. In Indiana and Ohio, the chamber of commerce led anti-labor activism or sponsored/worked closely with stand-alone right-to-work organizations. Other states witnessed splits or limited contact between mainstream employer associations and right-to-work groups. Even in Ohio, where the chamber of commerce coordinated the right-to-work campaign and several large manufacturers participated, some local chamber affiliates refused to participate, and the campaign struggled to reach out beyond an insular group of business leaders.

Connecting with political allies also proved more challenging than anticipated for employers. Ohio Republican officials saw employers' entry into contentious political debates as potentially damaging to the ticket and were slow to get behind them. In Wisconsin (and Illinois), just when right-to-work organizations formed and sought restrictions, their likely political allies shied away.

Across the region more generally, Michigan stood out mainly because of the dominance of a large, far-sighted union in the UAW, as noted earlier. With the UAW's support and influence, the state AFL-CIO had comparatively little problem putting up a united front on labor issues. In the 1950s, the liberal–labor coalition forestalled anti-labor initiatives in the state legislature with the veto threat of a popular Democratic governor. Anti-labor organizations, which made some inroads in the state, struggled to gain traction, particularly after the 1958 elections when Republicans were less willing to engage them. While Michigan combined strength at the bargaining table with a well-organized liberal–labor coalition in politics, this was not the norm. The more common pattern was that of disorganization and disinterest by unions and their allies. In Illinois, the building trades unions in Chicago benefitted from handshake relationships with the Democratic machine while industrial unions and the AFL-CIO's COPE were kept on the sidelines, save for big elections. Right-to-work efforts faded in Illinois due to countermovement divisions, but the state labor movement was also deeply divided and failed to coalesce around public-sector rights for another two decades.

Three patterns stand out when placing the campaigns in comparative perspective. First, there was no magic bullet or single route for labor influence. Unions used insider and outsider strategies to advance and defend labor rights, though their success was contingent on the splintering of employer opposition and the presence of resourceful local activists or a push from far-sighted national organizations that could circumvent otherwise weak state labor federations. Second, and following this last point, union influence can only be understood in relation to the employer-led countermovements trying to curb labor. The business-labor dynamic differs from most movement-countermovement pairs. Employers and their associations have built-in advantages and relationships with the state. Whereas patronage organization of parties mostly limited labor's political outlook, it did not prevent basic exchange relationships with employers. Yet when business moved from the quiet politics of insider influence to more contentious public issues, they struggled with many of the same issues facing labor. Here the interaction of the opposing movements mattered. When unions encountered a smoothly run employer countermovement, they were ill-prepared to stop it.

Third, state labor movements often lacked many of the key ingredients social movement researchers identify as necessary for success. Size alone did not ensure consistent influence or even acceptance when allies were few and infighting often spilled over into messy public disputes. As Democratic pollster Louis Harris & Associates described labor and the left's potential in Ohio politics, it was a "sleeping giant," but one who was rarely aroused. Favorable political opportunities and strong organization were not a given at the peak of union membership in the 1950s, but were highly variable, contributing to the mixed showing of unions in chapters 3–5.

Conclusion

This chapter examined the state of right-to-work and public-sector collective bargaining after the contention in the Midwest in the late 1950s and considered the experience of Michigan and Illinois, the two other large industrial states in the region. While right-to-work slowed in part due to the hesitancy of employers and their associations, public-sector organizing took off the following decade in conjunction with civil rights activism. The experience of Midwestern states was uneven here despite the considerable size and resources of state labor movements.

I find that the routes to union influence were multiple and context contingent. State labor movements often lacked many of the key ingredients for political influence. Unions succeeded by cultivating influential political allies and building a broad coalition and because of the missteps of their opponents. While state labor movements often lacked in expertise and outlook, the more basic organizational problem was deep and often dysfunctional divisions between building trades and industrial unions. This made forging connections with political or community allies difficult. It also opened the door for employer initiatives to curb unions throughout the region.

At the peak of union strength, labor often struggled to put its sizeable resources to work in ways that brought in important community allies and secured the consistent support of state actors. Considering the distinct insider and coalition routes for union success, labor's political operations in the states generally became more sophisticated following the 1950s, particularly among the new or recently active public-sector unions. The ability to form wide-ranging coalitions proved more difficult. I conclude in the next chapter by considering these two routes for unions today in the context of an active, well-funded, conservative countermovement.

7

Labor Rights in the Era of Union Decline

This book revisited labor at its peak by following campaigns over right-to-work laws and public-sector collective bargaining rights in the industrial Midwest in the late 1950s. My focus on labor conflict during the 1950s departs from popular and academic treatments of the period that emphasize consensus, an accord between capital and labor in collective bargaining, or the conservative drift and bureaucratization of the labor movement. I bring the focus down from unions and national politics to consider the variegated mix of labor, allies, and opponents across states. In doing so, I provide new insights on the limits of union power in the mid-twentieth century, anti-union mobilization by employers, what it took for unions to fight back when times were good, and what it means for the long road ahead. In this concluding chapter, I revisit the general findings of the book and consider how important weaknesses unions exhibited in the 1950s matter in the era of union decline.

Labor at Its Peak

The labor movement at its twentieth-century peak was a mixed bag. I have emphasized the underperformance of labor in the industrial heartland. This should not discount the real and important gains unions achieved. The early postwar decades were exceptional not because America was great during these years—the past is never as good as we would like to remember—but because a confluence of factors combined to produce significant economic growth and a more equitable distribution of the rewards than we have seen before or after. The increase in earnings for those on the middle and lower ends of the economic ladder were especially dramatic. Unions were the driving force behind these gains. Research emphasizing an accord between unions and large firms gets this part right. The achievements of unions in collective bargaining, in the industrial Midwest in particular, were considerable and improved the life chances of millions of workers and their families.

Heartland Blues. Marc Dixon, Oxford University Press (2020). © Oxford University Press.
DOI: 10.1093/oso/9780190917036.001.0001.

With times seemingly good, however, unions often struggled to parley their numbers and successes in collective bargaining into political influence and social acceptance. Part of this reflected the diminished ambitions of the labor movement. As much critical labor scholarship has shown, many unions were on the retreat by the 1950s, trying to hold on to their wartime gains but not expand them or seek out new constituencies. This narrowing of labor's outlook proved costly. Labor's social change efforts were soon eclipsed by an insurgent civil rights movement, which private-sector unions mostly ignored (or worse), and then by the flowering of New Left movements in the following decades. The labor dynamo of the 1930s and 1940s had slowed down. When union decline began to accelerate later in the twentieth century and unions were in dire need of allies, these social movements unsurprisingly struggled to find common cause with labor.

Neither the positive nor more critical perspectives on postwar labor relations explain the mixed showing by unions in the industrial heartland in the 1950s. It was more than diminished ambitions. Unions were slowed by messy infighting, limited interest from their likely political allies, and, importantly, business opposition. While many large firms had abandoned direct attacks on unions by the 1950s, they still supported under-the-radar activities such as the funding of other labor adversaries, including nascent think tanks and conservative media. Some never relented despite the narrowing of labor's goals. Moreover, stable collective bargaining with large firms did not preclude intense—and, indeed, violent—labor conflicts with smaller (though still very big) manufacturers like Kohler and Perfect Circle. The concentration of basic industry in the Midwest coupled with the backing of the New Deal and wartime state, forces that helped unions to become so big in the first place, did not eliminate the substantial resistance of small producers, agrarian interests, and politicians who saw little value in attaching their electoral fortunes to labor. Employers recognized these weaknesses; they played upon union divisions and recruited workers to help make their case against unions. While big auto and steel firms stayed quiet on right-to-work, many large firms took a more active role, and state business federations worked hard to make anti-unionism a viable political strategy in the industrial heartland.

Part of this was labor's own doing. Deep divisions between industrial unions and the building trades complicated everything. Infighting diminished labor's size advantage by limiting coordination, and messy disputes often spilled over into the public and put labor in a bad light. The national

AFL-CIO merger in 1955 did not solve this. Nor did the heavy concentration of the more progressive and politically active CIO unions in the industrial Midwest. The looming presence of the UAW in Michigan pushed the state labor movement to adopt a more progressive worldview. More often, however, state labor movements in the Midwest were marked by internal conflict and significant backlash from the older AFL unions. While many unions and state labor federations saw little value in coalitions and outreach, those that did were sometimes too disorganized to connect with potential allies outside of the labor movement.

Beyond intra-movement conflict, unions' most likely political allies were themselves disorganized and often disinterested in collaboration. Parties organized along patronage lines were cool to the industrial unions, while AFL unions proved less threatening. This meant that even as CIO unions scored big gains at the bargaining table, they struggled to win over, or even fit in, the local political contexts of the Midwest. The national alliance between the labor movement and the Democratic Party played out unevenly in the region despite the heavy concentration of union membership. Indeed, there was a substantial disconnect between labor's real political strength in the postwar era, headed by the industrial union–Democratic Party coalition in Congress, and its state and local organization characterized by infighting, ambivalent and unreliable political allies, and substantial employer opposition. Whether due to labor's own doing or forces outside of their control, the varied configurations of labor organization, opponents, and allies across the region posed significant obstacles to union influence at labor's peak.

Left to their own devices, most state labor movements lacked good solutions to stem the anti-union tide at the end of the 1950s. One thing that saved labor was that employers were also disorganized. When employers embraced a more strident and public opposition to unions in the industrial heartland, some of their key political allies were less inclined to go along; employers found the anti-labor coalition difficult to sustain. Employer mobilization in the Midwest had other consequences. It pushed the national labor movement to become more involved in state struggles, and it hastened merger negotiations between recalcitrant state labor factions. Taken together with the electoral fallout in 1958, this pushed most employer associations in the Midwest to back away from right-to-work and to pursue less controversial or public strategies to limit labor rights. Even after their big year, however, unions still struggled with coordination and outreach and were slow to advance a pro-labor vision or much policy. Public-sector collective bargaining rights developed unevenly in the region following the break-through in Wisconsin in 1959.

What worked then for labor in the state campaigns? The social movement framework I employed suggests there are multiple potential routes to campaign success, but that groups typically need strong political backing or effective organizations, and ideally both, to navigate them. They also have to find ways to counter their opponents' political mobilization. When put to the test in right-to-work and public-sector collective bargaining campaigns, unions found some success using both insider and outsider strategies. One route relied on a broad community coalition, mostly in the absence of support from political officials. The other relied heavily on political opportunities, and particularly the slow cultivation of political allies. Both routes required a break from the routine in order to overcome divided labor federations and push disinterested politicians. In Ohio, this meant the involvement of the national AFL-CIO, a sophisticated public relations firm, and the systematic recruitment of both labor and non-labor constituencies to sway the public on right to work. In Wisconsin, the generally quiet legislative work relied on unusually resourceful local activists—activists who circumvented a relatively weak state labor federation and helped to rebuild a moribund Democratic Party. Both routes also benefitted from the splintering of labor opposition at the end of the 1950s.

The successful insider route stood out from most labor political action in that the growing ties between union activists and officeholders in Wisconsin were not facilitated by existing party organizations and state labor federations. Instead, local public-sector activists were one of the key players to help rebuild the Wisconsin Democratic Party from scratch while the state labor federations were slower to come around. These activists slowly created their own political opportunities and found themselves in the right place at the right time as the conservative opposition fractured.

The labor coalition fighting right-to-work in Ohio broke from past practice in two important ways. First, it removed unions, and particularly union leaders, as the face of the campaign. Second, the participation of respected civic and religious groups brought what unions often struggled to attain: legitimacy in the community. Religious groups, which both labor and business had courted to varying degrees in the early postwar years, were especially important. Most sided with labor. They provided a critical buffer from the sensational reports of union corruption coming out of the McClellan Committee. Taken together, this turned the typical business campaigning against unions upside down. It brought labor closer to the mainstream of social life and, at its best, put business on the defensive as a greedy special interest.

The coalition rattled business leaders like Lemuel Boulware because it portrayed anti-union activity as self-serving and a "big business" project. Political mobilization by business came to be seen as an overreach. Unions had a hard time convincing the public of this on their own. It took others to make the case. Scholarship on collective action frames demonstrates the importance of the signifying work of social movements and how they produce and maintain meaning for members and other audiences. This kind of meaning making is constrained by material conditions, including the status of those making public claims about labor. The coalition changed how the labor side could talk about right-to-work in part by letting others do it.

There were limits. Most of the labor–community ties proved to be arm's length. It was a coalition born out of crisis and did not last much beyond the campaign. It fits what Jane McAlevey has described as a "mobilizing" model of contemporary organizing, one heavy on expertise and strategic messaging but less so mass-based organizing. This model is unlikely to generate enduring ties and influence, and it didn't. Still, the Ohio coalition proved an effective pushback to business mobilization at the end of the 1950s. It allowed labor to reach a broader audience and to put itself closer to the center of the community. This much rightly frightened the business community.[1]

Both routes to union influence would face enormous challenges in the coming decades. But the 1950s is more than an interesting side story. The weaknesses of the postwar labor movement outlined here were never solved; they became huge liabilities in the following decades as the economic environment worsened and employers regrouped. Moreover, the 1950s story matters because not only did labor fail to crack the Sunbelt, it never really conquered the industrial Midwest, where most union members resided in the mid-twentieth century. This diminished union influence within the Democratic Party and in society. Labor's political mobilizations never bore as much fruit as activists hoped and expected. Indeed, union successes in 1958 could not move the needle on labor's prized goal of Taft-Hartley reform. Congress instead passed the Landrum Griffin Act in 1959, which sought to reel in union malfeasance and imposed significant reporting obligations on unions. Not even the anti-Goldwater liberal landslide of 1964 could secure Taft-Hartley reform.[2]

The state labor policies considered here are also important. Conservatives today understand this well. Right-to-work laws are shown to dampen turnout

for Democratic candidates, to make it more difficult for unions to o_
and to embolden employers in their dealings with labor and like-minded social movements. The public sector has been one of the only sources of union
growth over the last half century, and formal collective bargaining rights
were central to this. Both right-to-work and public-sector collective bargaining rights help explain variation in union membership across the United
States over the last half century.[3]

Coping with Decline

The percentage of workers belonging to unions had been in decline since the
mid-1950s, but this accelerated and reached crisis levels in the 1970s and
1980s. Increased global competition, stagflation and financial crisis, and an
emboldened employer opposition appeared to push a sputtering labor movement off the cliff, starting the nosedive in union membership and organizing
effectiveness. The 1970s is thus often seen as the beginning of the end for
the labor movement. While there are many culprits for labor's steep decline,
it was during these years that the obstacles to union influence so evident in
the 1950s—union infighting, limited outreach, ambivalent political allies,
and an inability to push back against powerful business interests—became
seemingly insurmountable. The labor movement worked to solve some of
these issues. The deep union divisions of the early postwar years, for example, subsided at least for a time. Other problems proved enduring and
more troubling. Indeed, labor's social and political isolation and their limited
response to employer mobilization came back to bite them as they sought
organizational and legislative remedies to industrial decline and the rising
anti-union tide.[4]

Membership losses were especially big for those unions rooted in the in-
dustrial Midwest. Five thousand steelworkers were laid off in Youngstown,
Ohio, in 1977, when Youngstown Sheet & Tube closed their biggest plant.
Similar scenes played out across the region with the recession of 1981–1982
hitting manufacturing especially hard. Industrial strongholds were gutted
of jobs and residents. Entire communities were upended. The UAW and
USW lost more than 400,000 members each just between 1979 and 1984.
Employment in the non-union sector grew in the following years while tradi-
tionally unionized industries declined. Union membership in manufacturing

was cut in half between the early 1970s and the early 1990s and then again between the 1990s and today.[5]

Plant closures, layoffs, and downsizing were only part of labor's problems. Facing increased competition and declining profits, employer militancy returned in force at the point of production. Large firms took a hard line with unions. Some firms baited unions into unwinnable strikes in the hopes of replacing the union altogether or at least getting big concessions out of them. Firms supported union decertification elections. The process, which allows workers to remove an existing union through an NLRB election, was used sparingly in the mid-twentieth century, but many firms began to actively encourage them in the 1970s and 1980s. Industrial unions were not the only targets. The Construction Users Anti-Inflation Roundtable, soon to be the Business Roundtable, made curbing the building trades unions a top priority; they pushed union shop construction firms to open up non-union subsidiaries and sought to eliminate laws that propped up wages in construction, including the Davis Bacon Act and its state equivalents in prevailing wage laws.[6]

Employer militancy on the ground was not at first tightly connected to Republican politics. Nixon, for example, sought to woo working-class whites and mostly took a soft approach with organized labor, sometimes to the frustration of his advisors. He welcomed the building trades unions into the White House and made Peter Brennan of the New York Building and Construction Trades Council his Secretary of Labor. In the states and the Midwest in particular, legislative action on right-to-work and prevailing wage never really took off in the 1970s and 1980s as state parties and employer associations did not align to make a concerted push. This changed with Reagan, at least in national politics, when he fired striking air traffic controllers in 1981 and signaled to all employers that labor was fair game. Reagan's actions combined with the recession left most unions shell-shocked. Union organizing was cut in half in the early 1980s and never returned to previous levels.[7]

If unions had to scrap it out when times were good, with mixed results, familiar problems now proved too much. Labor's social and political isolation meant that there were few allies to count on when employers cracked down. The experience of labor in the industrial Midwest is instructive. Increased employer militancy mostly led to reduced strike activity, though some unions fought back and waged what, in retrospect, were spectacular defensive struggles. In the 1980s and 1990s, bitter fights at Hormel, Caterpillar, and Bridgestone-Firestone among other manufacturers exploded into wide-ranging corporate campaigns. Unions expanded the scope of conflict by targeting diverse stakeholders from every angle and seeking out a variety of community allies. The campaigns were by most accounts state of the art; they even inspired non-labor social movements to adopt similar strategies in the 1990s and 2000s. That the labor efforts mostly failed is perhaps not surprising given the times. But the massive efforts drew a limited public response, sometimes sparking significant community opposition, though mostly in-difference. Unions failed to capture the public within the industrial heartland or to put the new realities of manufacturing marked by worker givebacks on the political agenda nationally.[8]

Limited outreach and community support were not always for a lack of trying. In 1981, AFL-CIO president Lane Kirkland organized a Solidarity Day on the Washington Mall. It stands out not just in terms of size—it is the largest public assembly the labor movement has ever organized, drawing over three hundred thousand people—but also composition. Union members stood side by side with environmentalists, civil rights activists, and women's rights activists. This suggested a different configuration of civil society, one where labor worked closely with the rights-based and "new" social movements rather than as distant partners or even adversaries. It proved to be an anomaly. Most unions were unable or unwilling to reach out despite other pushes from the top of the labor movement. After the first contested election in AFL-CIO history in 1995, John Sweeney's New Voice leadership promised to bring a new era of labor activism marked by increased orga-nizing and outreach to non-labor constituencies. Organizing levels did not increase in the aggregate despite many innovative efforts. There is no cen-tralized data source on union outreach, but studies on a host of labor-based coalition efforts (e.g., in organizing, striking, and other campaigns) suggest it remains infrequent despite the desperate need for allies. The next organiza-tional upheaval, when several large unions headed by the SEIU left the AFL-CIO in 2005 to form the Change to Win Federation, did not change this.[9]

Labor's political efforts were somewhat stable across decades of decline, though clearly not up to the task of countering the employer offensive. Amid the hollowing out of the industrial heartland and during a period that witnessed an explosion of other non-labor interest groups, union influence within state Democratic Parties surprisingly held steady over the last decades of the twentieth century. Some industrial unions and state labor federations declined in influence, while other segments became more influential and better at state politics, particularly public-sector unions and teacher associations, whose members are distributed commensurate with population within states. This, too, played out unevenly. For example, in Ohio, an already pluralist labor field grew more unwieldy, complicating ties with a disorganized Democratic Party. In Michigan, the UAW–Democratic Party coalition was resilient for some time as labor and party leaders strategically adapted to industrial decline.[10]

Nationally unions remained influential in the Democratic Party for candidate selection in presidential elections. Garnering support on labor issues in Congress was more difficult. By the 1990s, the AFL-CIO, which had supported free trade well into the decline years, found itself on the wrong side of the push for trade liberalization. The NAFTA vote in 1993 was a public embarrassment for the labor movement. The labor movement was uniform in its opposition and the bill lacked widespread public support. The Clinton administration was nevertheless able to portray labor's opposition as "anti-growth, obstructionist, and dangerously out of step with global realties." It convinced large numbers of Democrats to support the bill so that it passed with a comfortable bipartisan majority. The inability to count on Democrats for critical votes was of course not new. One constant across several decades and spanning both relatively high and low levels of union density, large Democratic majorities have not been enough to pass *pro-labor* reforms. Marick Masters and John Delaney attribute this to the labor movement's inability to connect its core issues with audiences beyond labor's immediate orbit. In the authors' assessment of union political activity in the 1990s and 2000s, they noted that "labor fails at the critical test: It simply does not inspire." The labor movement has been unable to develop and champion ideas that resonate beyond union households.[11]

The consequences of union insularity, which slowed the labor movement in the 1950s when it really was big, are more ominous today. Most Republican legislators are now openly hostile toward unions. Beginning in the early 2000s, organizations on the right, including Americans for Prosperity (AFP) began to take on the anchoring role in state Republican parties that unions sometimes held with Democrats. AFP along with other Koch-related organizations and traditional business associations, including the chamber of commerce, have been successful in pushing Republicans to the right on economic issues and peeling away what little support there was for labor. The increased focus on state politics by the right in recent decades has given them a stranglehold on state legislatures. While challenges to redistricting continue, the sway of conservative anti-labor Republicans, particularly in the Midwest, is strong. In a post–Citizens United era of unlimited spending, the right's financial and organizational infrastructure is robust and outpaces labor in most respects. Indeed, unlike the 1950s, the ties between pro-business organizations and state Republican parties appear much more in sync. Considering just the pro-business organizations in the Koch network, their balance of national funding and support alongside local expertise, something unions have long struggled with, is impressive.[12]

The recent wave of state legislative restrictions on unions in the 2000s and 2010s—right-to-work, curbs on public-sector bargaining and prevailing wage—was pushed by Republicans now much farther to the right and working in lockstep with pro-business associations. This time unions were much smaller, but their difficulties were not new. In most cases labor struggled to mobilize enough community or political support to push back against a tightly connected right-wing corporate network. The early returns are not promising for labor. Studies on the recent policy setbacks find corporate and conservative political organizations have been highly effective in lobbying state legislatures, while state differences in union membership, public opinion on labor, and even the economic disruptions posed by the Great Recession had little or no impact.[13]

What Now?

Attacks on unions shows no signs of abating. This has caused much handwringing and serious debate within the labor movement. Yet union responses to contemporary anti-labor mobilization, including the spate of anti-labor legislative initiatives that seemingly turned the Midwest upside down at the beginning of the 2010s, have not changed all that much from the campaigns described in this book. This despite the enormous challenges those familiar union strategies face today.

The recent battles in the Midwest show some promise but also familiar limits. In 2011, the labor-backed coalition convinced Ohio voters to reject a law stripping public-sector collective bargaining rights. In now Deep Red Missouri, voters in 2018 similarly rejected a right-to-work law passed by the state legislature. Nearly four times as many people voted against the measure as there are union members in the state. Following the successful coalition script of the late 1950s, unions in both of these contests came together early;

they recruited thousands of volunteers to knock on doors, including many from beyond the labor movement. They emphasized issues bigger than labor unions. In Ohio, activists singled out the heroes—nurses and firefighters—and mostly avoided the word "union." This kind of broad-based, well-funded, and organized pushback to anti-labor policies proved far more effective than the *proactive* citizens' initiative for labor rights that was voted down in Michigan in 2012, or the long, drawn-out struggle that ultimately pitted unions in a one-on-one contest with Wisconsin governor Scott Walker in 2011 and 2012, and in a more muted fashion in 2015. Reducing conflicts over labor rights to unions versus the legislature or unions versus a public official was a successful strategy for employers and anti-labor politicians in the 1950s when unions were big, and it remains so today with unions much weaker.[14]

Even labor's successful ground games in Ohio and Missouri exhibited familiar problems. Labor outspent their opponents by a wide margin in both cases. The resources for such challenges are dwindling, a problem made worse by the 2018 Supreme Court decision in *Janus v. AFSCME*. In addition, anti-labor forces understand that making unions commit resources to fight off restrictive legislation is a partial victory in itself, as these funds could otherwise be directed toward new organizing and, especially, electoral politics. The successful referendums also shied away from making a case for unions in their own right. The more sophisticated campaigns waged by business and labor in the 1950s likewise took this track. Strategic decisions to minimize group identity are not unique to business–labor conflict. However, while this type of outreach strategy and framing of conflict poses little problem for the business community, the implications for labor are more complicated. To be effective and to counter employer influence, unions need to mobilize their members or at least retain the threat of direct action by members. Removing unions from the face of labor rights campaigns is at odds with this basic need. Such efforts are unlikely to generate a lasting pro-labor political movement or to ensure union legitimacy.

What then? As unions have struggled to fend off attacks over the last decade, the inklings of a way forward have begun to emerge. From fast food workers' Fight for 15 and related minimum wage campaigns, to a spate of teacher strikes, first in Chicago and then across several red states from Kentucky to Oklahoma, unions have put collective bargaining rights alongside broader political demands. The recent teacher strikes marked a three-decade high in the number of workers involved in major work stoppages of one thousand workers or more. This new spurt of militancy stands out not just in sheer numbers. Many of the efforts were marked by far-reaching community coalitions. Rather than recruiting allies to fend off attacks in moments of crisis, activists have worked together with community partners from the outset to formulate demands and a broader vision of what unions can be, practicing what advocates have begun to call "bargaining for the common good." In a promising development, and perhaps relatedly, unions have become more popular in recent years, particularly with young people.[15]

The path forward remains murky. Some of the recent strikes have occurred in the absence of collective bargaining rights, and it is not clear if workers can build on-the-job actions to create more durable means of influence. What is clear is that there is no magic bullet. The new and exciting work by unions and their allies still requires significant resources, even if its potential rests more on people power than union coffers. It will still be shaped by, and sometimes run up against, the peculiarities of local and regional politics. Moreover, business organizations are already pushing a variety of legal strategies to undercut the new union activism. If this model takes off, however, it will be something truly new. Even at the height of their powers in the 1950s, unions struggled to make a case for labor rights as part of the public interest.

Notes

Preface

1. Marc Dixon, "Movements, Countermovements, and Policy Adoption: The Case of Right-to-Work Activism," *Social Forces* 87, no. 1 (September 2008): 473–500; Marc Dixon, "Union Threat, Countermovement Organization, and Labor Policy in the States, 1944–1960," *Social Problems* 57, no. 2 (May 2010): 157–174.
2. See David Brady, Regina S. Baker, and Ryan Finnigan, "When Unionization Disappears: State-Level Unionization and Working Poverty in the United States," *American Sociological Review* 78, no. 5 (2013): 872–896; Richard B. Freeman, Eunice Han, David Madland, and Brendan V. Duke, "How Does Declining Unionism Affect the American Middle Class and Intergenerational Mobility?" National Bureau of Economic Research working paper 21638 (October 2015); James Feigenbaum, Alexander Hertel Fernandez, and Vanessa Williamson, "From the Bargaining Table to the Ballot Box: Political Effects of Right to Work Laws," National Bureau of Economic Research working paper 24259 (January 2018, revised February 2019); Jake Rosenfeld, *What Unions No Longer Do* (Cambridge, MA: Harvard University Press, 2014); Bruce Western and Jake Rosenfeld, "Unions, Norms, and the Rise in U.S. Wage Inequality," *American Sociological Review* 76, no. 4 (August 2011): 513–537.
3. Richard B. Freeman and James L. Medoff, *What Do Unions Do?* (New York: Basic Books, 1984).

Chapter 1

1. See Gordon Lafer, "The Legislative Attack on American Wages and Labor Standards, 2011–2012," Economic Policy Institute (October 31, 2013), Briefing Paper #364; Jason Stein and Patrick Marley, *More Than They Bargained for: Scott Walker, Unions, and the Fight for Wisconsin* (Madison: University of Wisconsin Press, 2013).
2. The Wisconsin Senate requires a quorum of twenty senators for any bill that involves spending money. Stein and Marley, *More Than They Bargained for.*
3. Marc Dixon, "Right-to-Work's Big Moment," *The Hill*, June 15, 2015. http://thehill.com/blogs/congress-blog/labor/244882-right-to-works-big-moment
4. Joseph A. McCartin, "The Radical Roots of Janus," *The American Prospect*, February 27, 2018; Michael McQuarrie, "The Revolt of the Rust Belt: Place and Politics in the Age of Anger," *The British Journal of Sociology* 68 (2017): S120–S152.
5. AFL-CIO president Richard Trumka summed up the Wisconsin experience by noting "public sector unions cannot live as islands in a non-union sea." When public-sector

unions came into their own, a third of private-sector workers belonged to unions. This compared to around 7 percent when public-sector union rights were gutted and when right-to-work laws and a host of other anti-labor measures impacting public- and private-sector workers alike gained steam in the region. The few empirical studies of the policy setbacks for unions find the coordinated effort of conservative think tanks and advocacy organizations to be highly consequential. Richard Trumka, speech at Labor Research Action Network Conference, Georgetown University Law Center, June 18, 2013; Theda Skocpol and Alexander Hertel-Fernandez, "The Koch Network and Republican Party Extremism," *Perspectives on Politics* 14, no. 3 (2016): 681–699.

6. For an overview of the research on union decline, see Dan Clawson and Mary Ann Clawson, "What Has Happened to the US Labor Movement? Union Decline and Renewal," *Annual Review of Sociology* 25 (August 1999): 95–119; Jack Fiorito, "The State of Unions in the United States," *Journal of Labor Research* 28, no. 1 (2007): 43–68; John Godard, "The Exceptional Decline of the American Labor Movement," *Industrial and Labor Relations Review* 63, no. 1 (2009): 82–108; Howard Kimeldorf, "Worker Replacement Costs and Unionization: Origins of the U.S. Labor Movement," *American Sociological Review* 78, no. 6 (2013): 1033–1062; Nelson Lichtenstein, *State of the Union* (Princeton, NJ: Princeton University Press, 2002); Jake Rosenfeld, *What Unions No Longer Do* (Cambridge, MA: Harvard University Press, 2014); Lane Windham, *Knocking on Labor's Door: Union Organizing in the 1970s and the Roots of a New Economic Divide* (Chapel Hill: University of North Carolina Press, 2017). On Reagan and the air traffic controllers as a turning point for organizing, see Daniel Tope and David Jacobs, "The Politics of Union Decline: The Contingent Determinants of Union Recognition Elections and Victories," *American Sociological Review* 74 (2009): 842–864.

7. Rosenfeld, *What Unions No Longer Do*; Joseph Varga, "Dispossession Is Nine-Tenths of the Law: Right-to-Work and the Making of the American Precariat," *Labor Studies Journal* 39, no. 1 (2014): 25–45.

8. For an example of the heavy role of the 1950s in framing contemporary understanding of inequality, see Robert Putnam's *Our Kids: The American Dream in Crisis* (New York: Simon & Schuster, 2016). On Trump and the nostalgia of the 1950s, see John Campbell, *American Discontent: The Rise of Donald Trump and the Decline of the Golden Age* (New York: Oxford University Press, 2018).

9. Jefferson Cowie, *The Great Exception* (Princeton, NJ: Princeton University Press, 2016), 154.

10. On union gains during this period, see Beth Rubin, "Class Struggle American Style: Unions, Strikes and Wages," *American Sociological Review* 51, no. 5 (1986): 618–633. References to the accord in the labor literature are often posed in contrast to unions' current shortcomings. See Andrew W. Martin and Marc Dixon, "Changing to Win? Threat, Resistance, and the Role of Unions in Strikes, 1984–2002," *American Journal of Sociology* 116, no. 1 (2010): 93–129.

11. Stephen Amberg, "The CIO Political Strategy in Historical Perspective: Creating a High-Road Economy in the Postwar Era," in *Organized Labor and American Politics, 1894–1994: The Labor-Liberal Alliance*, ed. Kevin Boyle (Albany, NY: SUNY Press,

1998), 159–194. Daniel Schlozman, *When Movements Anchor Parties: Electoral Alignments in American History* (Princeton, NJ: Princeton University Press, 2015); John Kenneth Galbraith, *American Capitalism: The Concept of Countervailing Power* (Boston: Houghton Mifflin, 1952). As Taylor Dark shows, this relationship continued to hold in national politics well after union decline had set in. See Dark's *The Unions and the Democrats: An Enduring Alliance* (Ithaca, NY: Cornell University Press, 1999).

12. Barry Eidlin, *Labor and the Class Idea in the United States and Canada* (Cambridge, UK: Cambridge University Press, 2018); Holly J. McCammon, "Disorganizing and Reorganizing Conflict: Outcomes of the State's Legal Regulation of the Strike Since the Wagner Act," *Social Forces* 72, no. 4 (1994): 1011–1049.

13. Judith Stepan-Norris and Maurice Zeitlin, *Left Out: Reds and America's Industrial Unions* (New York: Cambridge University Press, 2003).

14. The American Institute for Free Labor Development is one example of joint labor–federal government involvement in the region. The institute trained union leaders and supported labor federations that aligned with American interests while working against those that did not. See Kim Scipes, "It's Time to Come Clean: Open the AFL-CIO Archives on International Labor Operations," *Labor Studies Journal* 25, no. 2(2000): 4–25.

15. Lichtenstein, *State of the Union*, 237; Stepan-Norris and Zeitlin, *Left Out*, 274.

16. Elizabeth A. Fones-Wolf, *Selling Free Enterprise* (Urbana: University of Illinois Press, 1994); Nelson Lichtenstein and Elizabeth Tandy Shermer, eds., *The Right and Labor in America* (Philadelphia: University of Pennsylvania Press, 2012); Kim Phillips-Fein, *Invisible Hands: The Businessmen's Crusade Against the New Deal* (New York: W.W. Norton & Company, 2010).

17. Reagan hosted GE's Sunday-night television show in the 1950s, but he also toured the country visiting GE plants and speaking to employees and their families. He described his time at the company as his "postgraduate education in political science." See Thomas W. Evans, *The Education of Ronald Reagan: The General Electric Years and the Untold Story of His Conversion to Conservatism* (New York: Columbia University Press, 2006), 38..

18. Stepan-Norris and Zeitlin, *Left Out*, 275.

19. Local communities and politics were upended by deindustrialization as much research has shown. See especially Josh Pacewiz, *Partisans and Partners: The Politics of the Post-Keynesian Society* (Chicago: The University of Chicago Press, 2016). What I show in this book is that clustering of capital-intensive industry and progressive unions in the mid-twentieth century was often not enough to win over industrial communities on labor issues.

20. Jane McAlevey makes a strong case for unions as social movements in *No Shortcuts: Organizing for Power in the New Gilded Age* (New York: Oxford University Press, 2016). David Meyer provides a standard definition of social movements that I believe most unions and labor federations fit: "collective and sustained efforts that challenge existing or potential laws, policies, norms, or authorities, making use of extrainstitutional as well as institutional political tactics." Charles Tilly's definition rests on the melding of three elements: a sustained campaign, use of the social

movement repertoire (special purpose associations, marches, vigils, etc.), and public displays of WUNC—worthiness, unity, numbers, and commitment. See David S. Meyer, *The Politics of Protest: Social Movements in America* (New York: Oxford University Press, 2007), 10; Charles Tilly and Lesley J. Wood, *Social Movements, 1768–2008* (Boulder, CO: Paradigm, 2009). On the increasing formalization of social movements in the twentieth century, see David S. Meyer and Sidney Tarrow, "A Movement Society: Contentious Politics for a New Century," in *The Social Movement Society*, ed. David S. Meyer and Sidney Tarrow (Lanham, MD: Rowman & Littlefield, 1998), 1–28.

21. Jill Quadagno, *One Nation Uninsured* (New York: Oxford University Press, 2005); Edward T. Walker, *Grassroots for Hire: Public Affairs Consultants in American Democracy* (New York: Cambridge University Press, 2014).

22. On the relative weakness of movements, see Paul Burstein, *American Public Opinion, Advocacy, and Policy in Congress: What the Public Wants and What It Gets* (New York: Cambridge University Press, 2014); Doug McAdam and Hilary Schaffer Boudet, *Putting Social Movements in Their Place: Explaining Opposition to Energy Projects in the United States, 2000–2005* (New York: Cambridge University Press, 2012); E. E. Schattschneider, *The Semisovereign People* (New York: Holt, Rinehart and Winston, 1960).

23. Other scholarly traditions also emphasize some of the same political, legal, and organizational factors I describe here. For example, the comparative politics/political economy literatures have provided valuable insight into how political institutions impact labor organization. See especially Bruce Western's *Between Class and Market: Postwar Unionization in the Capitalist Democracies* (Princeton, NJ: Princeton University Press, 1997). But there is an analytical trade-off. Sweeping national comparisons emphasize institutions but offer much less on mobilization and process, though Thelen's recent work is a notable exception. See Kathleen Thelen, *Varieties of Liberalization and the New Politics of Social Solidarity* (New York: Cambridge University Press, 2014). By contrast, social movement theory is well equipped to understand the mobilization of unions and their opponents across the distinct local contexts I examine.

24. Doug McAdam's seminal work on the American civil rights movement saw a shift in political opportunities as capable of altering the "calculations and assumptions on which the political establishment is structured." This kind of shift—a new ally coming around to a movement's issue or favorable legislation making it easier to organize— can provide incentives for mobilization by increasing the prospects of social movement success. McAdam identifies four broad dimensions of opportunity: the relative openness of the political system; the stability of elite alignments and coalitions; the presence of elite allies; and the state's capacity for repression. Some opportunities are dynamic and can change quickly, such as the salience of a particular issue for legislators and their willingness to align with a social movement. Movements, of course, have imperfect information and do not always recognize such changes in the political establishment until it is too late. On political opportunity theory, see Doug McAdam, *Political Process and the Development of Black Insurgency, 1930–1970*

(Chicago: University of Chicago Press, 1999); David S. Meyer, "Protest and Political Opportunities," *Annual Review of Sociology* 30 (2007): 125–145. On the political mediation model, see Edwin Amenta, *When Movements Matter: The Townsend Plan and the Rise of Social Security* (Princeton, NJ: Princeton University Press, 2006).

25. Amberg, "The CIO Political Strategy in Historical Perspective"; Dark, *The Unions and the Democrats*, 28; David R. Mayhew, *Placing Parties in American Politics: Organization, Electoral Settings, and Government Activity in the Twentieth Century* (Princeton, NJ: Princeton University Press, 1986).

26. Early insight on social movement organizations comes from resource mobilization theory and the work of John McCarthy and Mayer Zald. In an influential 1977 article, they identified a move toward, and clear benefits from, the professionalization of social movement organizations (John D. McCarthy and Mayer N. Zald, "Resource Mobilization and Social Movements: A Partial Theory," *American Journal of Sociology* 82, no. 6 (1977): 1212–1241). Several studies have extended this work to the political process. One approach has simply been to show an association between social movement presence (e.g., number and/or size of organizations in a jurisdiction) and the likelihood of pro-movement policies while accounting for political opportunities and other relevant factors. On the influence of social movement organization across different stages of the policy process, see Sarah A. Soule and Brayden G. King, "The Stages of the Policy Process and the Equal Rights Amendment, 1972–1982," *American Journal of Sociology* 111, no. 6 (2006): 1871–1909. Holly McCammon addresses the more basic problem by identifying the organizational characteristics that enable movements to understand changes in the political environment in the first place and develop their strategies accordingly. Holly J. McCammon, *The U.S. Women's Jury Movements and Strategic Adaptation: A More Just Verdict* (New York: Cambridge University Press, 2012). See also Kenneth T. Andrews, "Social Movements and Policy Implementation: The Mississippi Civil Rights Movement and the War on Poverty, 1965 to 1971," *American Sociological Review* 66, no. 1 (2001): 71–95; Marshal Ganz, *Why David Sometimes Wins* (New York: Oxford University Press, 2009).

27. Lichtenstein, *State of the Union*.

28. Joel Rogers, "Divide and Conquer: Further 'Reflections on the Distinctive Character of American Labor Laws,'" *University of Wisconsin Law Review* (1990): 1–147. Stepan-Norris and Southworth find interorganizational conflict and competition to positively impact union growth over the twentieth century. See Judith Stepan-Norris and Caleb Southworth, "Rival Unionism and Membership Growth in the United States, 1900 to 2005," *American Sociological Review* 75, no. 2 (2010): 227–251.

29. Gilbert J. Gall, "Thoughts on Defeating Right-to-Work: Reflections on Two Referendum Campaigns," in *Organized Labor and American Politics, 1894–1994: The Labor-Liberal Alliance*, ed. Kevin Boyle (Albany, NY: SUNY Press, 1998), 195–216.

30. Cedric de Leon, *The Origins of Right-to-Work: Antilabor Democracy in Nineteenth-Century Chicago* (Ithaca, NY: ILR Press, 2015).

31. Beginning with the work of David Snow and colleagues, scholars have systematically analyzed how social movements package and construct meaning for a variety of audiences, often as movements attempt to recruit and mobilize potential supporters.

See especially David A. Snow, E. Burke Rochford, Jr., Steven K. Worden, and Robert D. Benford, "Frame Alignment Processes, Micromobilization, and Movement Participation," *American Sociological Review* 51, no. 4 (1986): 464–481. Like research on political opportunity and social movement organization, scholars have moved from showing how framing matters for mobilization to show its influence on a variety of social movement outcomes, including policy. Daniel Cress and David Snow's multisite ethnography of activism on homelessness illustrates how framing works in combination with social movement organization and tactical choices to influence municipal policies. The specific characteristics of resonant frames also vary by audience and setting. For example, frames designed to motivate one's constituency to protest may be unlikely to sway policymakers or draw in other bystanders. See Daniel M. Cress and David A. Snow, "The Outcomes of Homeless Mobilization: The Influence of Organization, Disruption, Political Mediation, and Framing," *American Journal of Sociology* 105, no. 4 (2000): 1063–1104. On strategic decisions to emphasize or minimize group identity in the framing of conflict, see Mary Bernstein, "Celebration and Suppression: The Strategic Uses of Identity by the Lesbian and Gay Movement," *American Journal of Sociology* 103 (1997): 531–565.

32. I view the availability of community allies as a dimension of political opportunity in that it potentially alters the political calculus of elected officials when dealing with labor. On strategies, I include coalitions and framing together as important and tightly related persuasive tools in the social movement repertoire. For labor, conveying labor rights as in the public interest often hinged on the willingness of non-labor actors to make this case. Connecting with other organizations in civil society and putting these organizations out in front of the issue helped them do this. Coalitions were thus more important for framing in this case than is typically treated in the social movement literature.

33. On movement-countermovement dynamics, see David Meyer and Suzanne Staggenborg, "Movements, Countermovements, and the Structure of Political Opportunity," *American Journal of Sociology* 101, no. 6 (1996): 1628–1660; Mayer N. Zald and Burt Useem, "Movement and Countermovement Interaction: Mobilization, Tactics, and State Involvement," *Social Movements in an Organizational Society*, ed. Mayer N. Zald and John McCarthy (New Brunswick, NJ: Transaction Books, 1987), 247–272.

34. Claus Offe and Helmut Wiesenthal, "Two Logics of Collective Action: Theoretical Notes on Social Class and Organizational Form," *Political Power and Social Theory* 1, no. 1 (1980): 67–115.

35. Brayden G. King and Nicholas Pearce, "The Contentiousness of Markets: Politics, Social Movements, and Institutional Change in Markets," *Annual Review of Sociology* 36 (2010): 249–267.

36. Simeon Alder, David Lagakos, and Lee Ohanian, "Competitive Pressure and the Decline of the Rust Belt: A Macroeconomic Analysis," National Bureau of Economic Research Working Paper 20538 (2014).

37. On the place of Wisconsin for the development of public-sector bargaining law, see Joseph E. Slater, *Public Workers: Government Employee Unions, the Law, and the*

State, 1900–1962 (Ithaca, NY: Cornell University Press, 2004). On civil rights-public sector organizing, see especially Larry Isaac and Lars Christiansen, "How the Civil Rights Movement Revitalized Labor Militancy," *American Sociological Review* 67 (2002): 722–746; Larry Isaac, Steve McDonald, and Greg Lukasik, "Takin' It from the Streets: How the Sixties Mass Movement Revitalized Unionization," *American Journal of Sociology* 112 (2006): 46–96.

38. See David T. Ellwood and Glenn Fine, "The Impact of Right-to-Work Laws on Union Organizing," *Journal of Political Economy* 95, no. 2 (1987): 250–273; James Feigenbaum, Alexander Hertel-Fernandez, and Vanessa Williamson, "From the Bargaining Table to the Ballot Box: Political Effects of Right to Work Laws," National Bureau of Economic Research working paper 24259 (January 2018, revised February 2019); David Jacobs and Marc Dixon, "Political Partisanship, Race, and Union Strength from 1970 to 2000: A Pooled Time-Series Analysis," *Social Science Research* 39, no. 6 (2010): 1059–1072; Gregory M. Saltzman, "Public Sector Bargaining Laws Really Matter: Evidence from Ohio and Illinois," Chapter 2 in Richard B. Freeman and Casey Ichniowski, eds., *When Public Sector Workers Unionize* (Chicago: NBER and University of Chicago Press, 1988).

39. Millions of African Americans moved to industrial areas in Midwest and West during the 1940s and had an important impact on many local labor movements despite their still relatively small share of the population. The space for black activism and leadership within industrial unions began to close with the onset of the Cold War and the expulsion of the key advocates for racial equality, namely communists, from the labor movement. See Robert Korstad and Nelson Lichtenstein, "Opportunities Found and Lost: Labor, Radicals, and the Early Civil Rights Movement," *The Journal of American History* 75, no. 3 (1988): 786–811.

40. Rory McVeigh, *The Rise of the Ku Klux Klan: Right-Wing Movements and National Politics* (Minneapolis: University of Minnesota Press, 2009).

41. On Progressive Era activism and politics, see Elisabeth Clemens, *The People's Lobby: Organizational Innovation and the Rise of Interest Group Politics in the United States, 1890–1925* (Chicago: The University of Chicago Press, 1997).

42. See especially Dietrich Rueschemeyer, "Can One or a Few Cases Yield Theoretical Gains?" Chapter 9 in *Comparative Historical Analysis in the Social Sciences*, ed. James Mahoney and Dietrich Rueschemeyer (New York: Cambridge University Press, 2003).

43. The three focal cases rely more heavily on primary materials, while the expanded case comparisons of Michigan and Illinois draw more from secondary histories.

Chapter 2

1. Many have challenged the consensus of the 1950s. Stanley Aronowitz provides an early critique of this view and labor's role. See *False Promises: The Shaping of American Working Class Consciousness* (New York: McGraw-Hill, 1973), Chapter 7. Still, public intellectuals of the period such as Daniel Bell saw ideological conflict as mostly

exhausted. With Soviet Communism exposed and delegitimated, it was assumed that liberals and conservatives tended to at least agree about the basic organization of society and the place of business, labor, and the state. Prominent theories of politics and labor relations during the period mirrored this harmony and veered toward pluralism, where multiple competing interest groups were argued to shape policy debates and a relative peace ensured smooth, institutionalized bargaining between labor and management. See Daniel Bell, *The End of Ideology* (Glencoe, IL: The Free Press, 1960). For examples of pluralism in politics and industrial relations, see Clark Kerr, ed., *Labor and Management in Industrial Society* (New York: Anchor, 1964); Nelson W. Polsby, "How to Study Community Power: The Pluralist Alternative," *Journal of Politics* 22 (1960): 474–484.

2. See David M. Kotz, *The Rise and Fall of Neoliberal Capitalism* (Cambridge, MA: Harvard University Press, 2015). The regulated capitalism of the postwar era was not of course limited to stable collective bargaining and the capital–labor accord. Significant state intervention—including the GI Bill, which subsidized home ownership—also facilitated upward social mobility for many.

3. See Jake Rosenfeld, *What Unions No Longer Do* (Cambridge, MA: Harvard University Press, 2014); Bruce Western and Jake Rosenfeld, "Unions, Norms, and the Rise in U.S. Wage Inequality," *American Sociological Review* 76 (2011): 513–537.

4. Mark S. Mizruchi, *The Fracturing of the American Corporate Elite* (Cambridge, MA: Harvard University Press, 2013).

5. John J. Sweeney and Karen Nussbaum, *Solution for the New Workforce* (Cabin John, MD: Seven Locks Press).

6. See Sameul Bowles, David Gordon, and Thomas Weisskopf, *Beyond the Wasteland: A Democratic Alternative to Economic* Decline (New York: Anchor Press, 1983). Bruce Nissen's review identifies union legitimacy (acceptance of unions by firms) and managerial authority as the key pieces of the accord, followed by firms agreeing to the union shop and automatic dues check-off (where permissible) and unions eliminating wildcat or "quickie" strikes. Union busting in the form of actively breaking strikes and organizing campaigns, while the norm before the New Deal and certainly in more recent decades, was abandoned as a business strategy during this period. See "A Post-World War II 'Social Accord?,'" in *U.S. Labor Relations, 1945–1989: Accommodation and Conflict*, ed. Bruce Nissen (New York: Garland, 1990), 173–205.

7. Stephen Amberg, "The CIO Political Strategy in Historical Perspective: Creating a High-Road Economy in the Postwar Era," in *Organized Labor and American Politics, 1894–1994: The Labor-Liberal Alliance*, ed. Kevin Boyle (Albany: State University of New York Press, 1998), 159–194.

8. Samuel Lubell, *The Future of American Politics* (New York: Harper, 1951), 179–180; C. Wright Mills, *The New Men of Power* (Urbana: University of Illinois Press, [1948] 2001) and "Letter to the New Left," *New Left Review* I (1960): 18–23.

9. Kotz, *The Rise and Fall of Neoliberal Capitalism*; Daniel Bell, "The Treaty of Detroit," *Fortune*, July (1950): 53. On the implications of the Treaty of Detroit for the labor movement, see Nelson Lichtenstein, *State of the Union* (Princeton, NJ: Princeton University Press, 2002).

10. Nissen, "A Post-World War II 'Social Accord'?"; Beth Rubin, "Class Struggle American Style: Unions, Strikes, and Wages," *American Sociological Review* 51 (1986): 618–633.

11. The anti-union consultant industry developed in the 1950s moved away from Pinkertons and the use of labor spies that dominated nineteenth- and early twentieth-century labor relations and developed sophisticated Human Relations departments and held captive audience meetings with workers to dissuade them from unionizing. See Paul Lipold and Larry Isaac, "Striking Deaths: Lethal Contestation and the 'Exceptional' Character of the American Labor Movement, 1870–1970," *International Review of Social History* 54 (2009): 167–205; Kim Phillips-Fein, *Invisible Hands: The Businessmen's Crusade Against the New* Deal (New York: W.W. Norton & Company, 2010).

12. A growing body of scholarship, mostly by historians, challenges the consensus by documenting the great lengths that business groups went to in order to undermine labor. See especially David M. Anderson, "'Things Are Different Down Here': The 1955 Perfect Circle Strike, Conservative Civic Identity, and the Roots of the New Right in the 1950s Industrial Heartland," *International Labor and Working-Class History* 74 (2008): 101–123; Elizabeth A. Fones-Wolf, *Selling Free Enterprise* (Urbana: University of Illinois Press, 1994); Phillips-Fein, *Invisible Hands*.

13. Howell John Harris, *The Right to Manage: Industrial Relations Policies of American Business in the 1940s* (Madison: University of Wisconsin Press, 1982).

14. Manning Dauer, "Recent Southern Political Thought," *Journal of Politics* 10 (1948): 327–353; Marc Dixon, "Limiting Labor: Business Political Mobilization and Union Setback in the States," *Journal of Policy History* 19 (2007): 313–344.

15. Melvin Dubofsky and Warren Van Tine, *John L. Lewis: A Biography* (Urbana: University of Illinois Press, 1986).

16. Pressman quote in Dixon, "Limiting Labor," 335.

17. Stepan-Norris and Zeitlin, *Left Out*, 273. See also Michael Goldfield on the failure of Operation Dixie and its lasting impact in his *The Decline of Organized Labor in the United States* (Chicago: University of Chicago Press, 1987).

18. Dan Clawson, *The Next Upsurge: Labor and the New Social Movements* (Ithaca, NY: ILR Press, 2003).

19. See Lemuel R. Boulware, "Big Industry in the Community: General Electric Assesses Community Relations," *Journal of Educational Sociology* 27 (Dec. 1953): 152–159. Boulware went on the speaking circuit in 1958 to urge political action by business. Quote from speech to American Society of Association Executives Annual Meeting, White Sulphur Springs, West Virginia, August 1958 in Box 14, Folder 4 of the Lemuel R. Boulware Papers, MS Collection 52, Rare Book & Manuscript Library, University of Pennsylvania.

20. Phillips-Fein, *Invisible Hands*.

21. See Joseph A. McCartin, "The Radical Roots of Janus," *The American Prospect*, February (2018); Joseph A. McCartin and Jean-Christian Vinel, "'Compulsory Unionism': Sylvester Petro and the Career of an Anti-Union Idea, 1957–1987," in *The Right and Labor in America*, ed. Nelson Lichtenstein and Elizabeth Tandy Shermer (Philadelphia: University of Pennsylvania Press, 2012), 226–251. Sylvester Petro,

The Labor Policy of the Free Society (New York: Ronald Press, 1957) and *The Kohler Strike: Union Violence and Administrative Law* (Chicago: H. Regnery Co., 1961).

22. For a discussion of business unionism, see Marc Dixon and Andrew W. Martin, "'We Can't Win This on Our Own': Unions, Firms, and the Mobilization of External Allies in Labor Disputes," *American Sociological Review* 77 (2012): 946–969.

23. George Meany speech to the National Association of Manufacturers, December 9, 1955; copyright AFL-CIO; Record Group 1–027, Series 10, Box 59, Folder 76, The George Meany Memorial AFL-CIO Archive; Special Collections and University Archives, University of Maryland Libraries.

24. Fones-Wolf, *Selling Free Enterprise*. General Electric executive J. J. Wuerthner's 1959 book sounded a similar alarm to the Chamber of Commerce, urging business to fight against a tightly organized group of labor leaders whose main objective had become the seizing of political power and control of government. See J. J. Wuerthner, *The Businessman's Guide to Practical Politics* (Chicago: H. Regnery Co., 1959). Wisconsin Chamber of Commerce official quoted in *Wisconsin City and County Union News*, January 1957, p. 1.

25. Amberg, "The CIO Political Strategy in Historical Perspective."

26. Fones-Wolf, *Selling Free Enterprise*.

27. Anderson, "Things Are Different Down Here."

28. On the growing Reuther obsession among the right, see Nelson Lichtenstein, *The Most Dangerous Man in Detroit: Walter Reuther and the Fate of American Labor* (New York: Basic Books, 1995), Chapter 16.

29. Mike Davis, *Prisoners of the American Dream* (London: Verso, 1986).

30. Marc Dixon, "Movements, Countermovements, and Policy Adoption: The Case of Right-to-Work Activism," *Social Forces* 87 (2008): 473–500.

31. Roscoe Born, "Labor Plans Drive in Congress on Right-to-Work," *The Wall Street Journal*, November 6, 1958, p. 6; Joseph E. Slater, *Public Workers: Government Employee Unions, the Law, and the State, 1900–1962* (Ithaca, NY: ILR Press, 2004), Chapter 6.

32. Licthenstein, *The Most Dangerous Man in Detroit*.

33. Davis, *Prisoners of the American Dream*.

Chapter 3

1. "Behind Closed Doors," *The Indianapolis Star*, Sunday, March 3, 1957, p. 5.

2. John Bartlow Martin, *Indiana: An Interpretation* (New York: Alfred A. Knopf, 1947).

3. John H. Fenton, *Midwest Politics* (New York: Holt, Rinehart and Winston, 1966); Robert S. and Helen Lynd, *Middletown: A Study in Contemporary American Culture* (New York: Harcourt, Brace, and Company, 1929); Rory McVeigh, *The Rise of the Ku Klux Klan: Right-Wing Movements in National Politics* (Minneapolis: University of Minnesota Press, 2009).

4. Indiana Republican Party Platform reprinted in Indiana State Industrial Union Council, *Legislative Report: 90th General Assembly*, (Indianapolis, Indiana, 1957).

During the 1950s, staunch conservatives like US Senator William Jenner had less influence over the state party than did moderate Governor George Craig, who controlled all of the patronage.

5. Fenton, *Midwest Politics*.

6. Melvin Kahn, *The Politics of American Labor: The Indiana Microcosm* (Carbondale: Southern Illinois University Labor Institute, 1970); David R. Mayhew, *Placing Parties in American Politics: Organization, Electoral Settings, and Government Activity in the Twentieth Century* (Princeton, NJ: Princeton University Press, 1986).

7. Kahn, *The Politics of American Labor*, 223.

8. Hugh M. Ayer, "Hoosier Labor in the Second World War," *Indiana Magazine of History* LIX (1963): 95–120; Statistical Abstract of the United States, Bureau of the Census (Washington, DC: U.S. Government Printing Office, 1956).

9. Letter from Otto Suhr to Carl Mullen, July 15, 1957, included in the Proceedings of the Seventy-Second Annual Convention of the Indiana State Federation of Labor; Kahn, *The Politics of American Labor*, 13; Indiana State Industrial Union Council, "Comprehensive History of Indiana AFL-CIO Merger Negotiations," in UAW President's Office: Walter P. Reuther Records, Box 310, Folder 1, Walter P. Reuther Library.

10. Indiana State Industrial Union Council, "Comprehensive History of Indiana AFL-CIO Merger Negotiations."

11. Fred W. Perkins, "A Drive on the Right-to-Work Front," *The Washington Daily News*, Thursday, December 13, 1956, p. 1.

12. See David Anderson's "'Things Are Different Down Here': The 1955 Perfect Circle Strike, Conservative Civic Identity, and the Roots of the New Right in the 1950s Industrial Heartland," *International Labor and Working-Class History* 74 (2008): 101–123.

13. "Little Labor War," *Wall Street Journal*, Tuesday, October 18, p. 1.

14. "Little Labor War," 11; "Outline of a Public Relations Program on Major Labor Issues for 1955," Box 139, National Association of Manufacturers records (Accession 1411), Hagley Museum and Library.

15. Stephen Noland, "Labor Loses Rights Under Its Own Rule," *Steuben Republican*, March 15, 1950, p. 2.

16. Bart Grabow, "'Right to Work' Is Pushing for New State Law," *The Indianapolis News*, February 27, 1956, p. 26; Hooser became the chair of the NRTWC offshoot the National Council for Labor's Rank and File in 1960. Group Research report on The National Right-to-Work Committee, 1962, retrieved from: http://www.prwatch.org/files/rtw_group_research.pdf

17. Miller stands out as a labor moderate compared to the leaders of other smaller (but still very large) manufacturers in the region. He is better known for bringing modern architecture to his hometown of Columbus and for his continued investment there as other firms left the Midwest in the latter twentieth century.

18. On INRTWC board members, see Indiana State Federation of Labor, *Legislative Bulletin*, February 1, 1957. Joseph Varga notes that Cummings in particular opposed the effort. See Joesph Varga, "Dispossession Is Nine-tenths of the Law: Right-to-Work

and the Making of the American Precariat," *Labor Studies Journal* 39 (2014): 25–45. On small business activism and Manion, see especially Rick Perlstein, *Before the Storm: Barry Goldwater and the Unmaking of the American Consensus* (New York: Farrar, Straus and Giroux, 2001), Chapter 1; Kim Phillips-Fein, *Invisible Hands: The Businessmen's Crusade against the New Deal* (New York: Norton, 2009), 81–86;

19. "Here's Way to Sounds Laws," *Nation's Business*, June 1957, pp. 42–46; ISFL *Legislative Bulletin*, February 1.

20. Executive Board Report, *Proceedings of the Seventy-Second Annual Convention of the Indiana State Federation of Labor*, 82.

21. This is in contrast to the Chamber of Commerce, who built on existing relationships and used personalized scripts when calling upon representatives. "Behind Closed Doors," 5; Kahn, *The Politics of American Labor*.

22. Testimony from ISFL *Legislative Bulletin*, February 15, 1957; W. L. White, "The Right-to-Work: Our Hottest Labor Issue," *Readers Digest*, August, 1958; "Who's Boss Around Here?," *The Indianapolis Star*, Friday, February 8, 1957, p. 16.

23. Interview with Robert S. Webb, p. 39. Conducted by David F. Tudor, June 17, 1973, Bloomington, Indiana, Indiana University Center for the Study of History and Memory, #73-18.

24. Between the 1955 and 1957 sessions, Diener felt out a potential run for governor but ended up going back into business after the 1957 session. He was critical in getting the Right-to-Work bill out of the House Labor Committee. On replacing a member of the committee who had fallen ill during the session, he later remarked, "I wanted the Right to Work bill on the floor and I wanted it passed . . . I didn't hold back any punches." Interview with George Diener, conducted by Jerry Handfield, June 20, 1978, Indianapolis, Indiana State Library, Rare Books and Manuscripts Division, p. 10,

25. "Right-to-Work Law Defended by Minister," *Chicago Daily Tribune*, Monday, April 28, p. A6; Edward W. Greenfield, *The Anatomy of a Wildcat* (National Right-to-Work Committee, Washington, DC, 1957).

26. Nobody ever discovered the shooter. The local union condemned it and offered a reward for the shooter's apprehension, but the damage was done. "Goon Riddles Trailer; Baby Is Near Death," *Chicago Daily Tribune*, Thursday, February 14, 1957, pp. 1 and 6.

27. Jack Averitt, "Battle on for Work Bill Votes," *Indianapolis News*, Tuesday, February 26, p. 2; ISFL *Legislative Bulletin*, March 1, 1957.

28. Roll Call votes from IUC *Legislative Report*, 36–40; Legislator information from the Indiana Legislator Database: http://legdb.iga.in.gov/about/

29. There are differing accounts of the ISFL attempt to undercut the IUC at the end. *The Indianapolis Star*'s political column *Behind Closed Doors* reported on March 3 that anonymous craft union leaders approached Right-to-Work supporters on the eve of the Senate vote, urging them to exempt craft unions from the bill, after which they would "throw their weight" behind the measure. This failed along with the public attempts to dilute the bill. Later that year the IUC's *Legislative Report* had a more sanguine interpretation of the actual amendment that was voted down, seeing it as an

attempt by union supporters to sink the entire bill by splitting craft and industrial unions (32).

30. "Behind Closed Doors," *The Indianapolis Star*, Sunday, March 3, 1957, p. 5.

31. Otto Suhr position on the merger, July 15, 1957, included in ISFL *Proceedings*; Letter from the ISFL Executive Board to George Meany, August 15, 1957, included in ISFL *Proceedings*.

32. Indiana State Industrial Union Council, "Comprehensive History of Indiana AFL-CIO Merger Negotiations."

33. NAM survey outlined in D. L. Mewhinney, "Memorandum to National Industrial Council," January 28, 1955, [Need Box/Folder] National Association of Manufacturers records (Accession 1411), Hagley Museum and Library. Labor testimony from ISFL *Legislative Bulletin*, February 15, 1957.

34. "Memorandum to National Industrial Council"; "Behind Closed Doors," 5.

35. Union Shop Authorization data are from the *Annual Reports* of the *National Labor Relations Board*, 1948–1951; interview with Dallas W. Sells, conducted by R. T. King, March 2, 1979, Bloomington, Indiana, Indiana University Center for the Study of History and Memory.

36. Dell Bush Johannesen, "Recent Decisions Concerning the Agency Shop," *North Carolina Law Review* 40 (1962): 605–618.

37. William Book quoted in Martin, *Indiana*, 260; "Here's Way to Sound Laws," 42.

Chapter 4

1. Richard O. Davies, *Defender of the Old Guard: John Bricker and American Politics* (Columbus: Ohio State University Press, 1993), 196; letter from Charles Hook to C. William O'Neill, July 17, 1958, C. William O'Neill Papers, Box 43, Ohio Historical Society.

2. Raymond Boryczka and Lorin Lee Cary, *No Strength without Union: An Illustrated History of Ohio Workers, 1803–1980* (Columbus: The Ohio Historical Society, 1982); Andrew Cayton, *Ohio: The History of a People* (Columbus: The Ohio State University Press, 2002); John H. Fenton, *Midwest Politics* (New York: Holt, Rinehart and Winston, 1966).

3. Louis Harris and Associates, "A Study of Issues and Candidates in Ohio," September 1958, p. 4.

4. Fenton, *Midwest Politics*, 137; Ohio still had 131 independent and often single-employer unions in 1960, the highest total in the region. See Leo Troy, *Trade Union Membership, 1897–1962* (New York: National Bureau of Economic Research, 1965).

5. Michael Bowen, "Addition through Division: Robert Taft, the Labor Vote, and the Ohio Senate Election of 1950," *Ohio Valley History* 5 (2005): 21–42.

6. Samuel Lubell, "How Taft Did It," *The Saturday Evening Post*, February 10, 1951.

7. Taft quote from "Post-Election Statement," in *Robert A. Taft Papers*, volume 3, ed. by Clarence E. Wunderlin, Jr. (Kent, OH: Kent State University Press, 1997–2006), 207; Lubell, "How Taft Did It," 32.

8. Fenton, *Midwest Politics;* Kenneth E. Gray, *A Report on Politics in Cincinnati* (Cambridge, MA: Joint Center for Urban Studies of the Massachusetts Institute of Technology and Harvard University, 1959).

9. Wages of production workers from Statistical Abstract of the United States, Bureau of the Census (Washington, DC: U.S. Government Printing Office, 1956).

10. Warren Van Tine, C. J. Slanicka, Sandra Jordan, and Michale Pierce, *In the Workers' Interest: A History of the Ohio AFL-CIO, 1958–1998* (Columbus: Center for Labor Research, Ohio State University, 1998).

11. Cayton, *Ohio: The History of a People,* 325; Van Tine et al., *In the Workers' Interest.*

12. "Businessman Tells: How to Beat Unions at the Polls," *US News & World Report,* May 11, 1956, pp. 117–121; Herschel C. Atkinson, *Unions and Political Action: The Ohio Story, A Primer for Businessmen* (Washington, DC: U.S. Chamber of Commerce, 1956), 9.

13. Michael James Zavacky, *Interest Groups in the Initiative Referendum Process* (PhD Dissertation, University of Pittsburgh, 1968).

14. While Building Trades' unions expressed reservations to the merger because of jurisdictional disputes, they expressed no such reservations to joining UOLO. The Carpenters were one of the bigger financial contributors to the campaign to defeat right-to-work. See Van Tine et al., *In the Workers' Interest.*

15. "Campaign Report to UOLO," November 18, 1958, Charles Baker Papers, Box 4, Walter P. Reuther Labor Archives; Zavacky, *Interest Groups in the Initiative Referendum Process.*

16. Columbus Area Chamber of Commerce Bulletin, March 31, 1958, in Ohio AFL-CIO Papers, Box 48, Ohio Historical Society.

17. "Freedom of Choice" flyer, Ohio Right to Work Campaign Committee, n.d., in Ohio AFL-CIO Papers, Box 48, Ohio Historical Society.

18. See Proceedings of the Second Annual Industrial Relations Conference, Industrial Union Department, AFL-CIO, June 17, 1958, p. 19. Campaign materials were also generated for specific demographics. For seniors, labor contrasted the prosperity of the 1950s to the vivid memories of the Depression, hard times brought on by business. For women, unions appealed to the pocket book and their standard of living. Each aimed to place unions at the center of a prosperous society

19. "Campaign Report to UOLO," November 18, 1958, Charles Baker Papers, Box 4, Walter P. Reuther Labor Archives.

20. "Campaign Report to UOLO."

21. Early outreach activities are described in UOLO's *Home Front* publication, particularly issues 3 and 4. *Home Front* issues retrieved from The Samuel Pollock Papers, Accession 111, Box 1, Walter P. Reuther Labor Archives.

22. Glen W. Miller and Stephen B. Ware, "Organized Labor in the Political Process: A Case Study of the Right-to-work Campaign in Ohio," *Labor History* 4 (1963): 51–67.

23. Atkinson, *Unions and Political Action;* Zavacky, *Interest Groups in the Initiative Referendum Process,* 35.

24. Richard O. Davies, *Defender of the Old Guard: John Bricker and American Politics* (Columbus: Ohio State University Press, 1993), 196; Letter from Charles Hook to

C. William O'Neill, July 17, 1958, C. William O'Neill Papers, Box 43, Ohio Historical Society.

25. Davies, *Defender of the Old Guard*.

26. Michael B. Hissam, *C. William O'Neill and the 1958 Right-to-Work Amendment* (Honors Thesis, Department of History, The Ohio State University, 2005).

27. Letter from Charles Hook to President Dwight D. Eisenhower, October 28, 1958, in the C. William O'Neill Papers, Box 43, Ohio Historical Society.

28. See Richard G. Zimmerman, *Call Me Mike: A Political Biography of Michael DiSalle* (Kent, OH: Kent State University Press, 2003).

29. Roscoe Born, "Ohio Bookies Expect Right-to-Work to Win, Offer Odds of 7 to 5," *The Wall Street Journal*, October 31, 1958, p. 1.

30. "Campaign Report to UOLO," November 18, 1958, Charles Baker Papers, Box 4, Walter P. Reuther Labor Archives.

31. Interview with Senator James McClellan, "Can the Labor Racketeer Be Stopped?" *US News & World Report*, October 10, 1958, pp. 53–57: "Beatings, Bombings, Shootings . . . What the McLellan Files Show," *US News & World Report*, October 10, 1958, pp. 60–65.

32. Transcript of O'Neill's televised address in Samuel Pollock Papers, Box 3, Walter P. Reuther Labor Archives.

33. OHRTW flyers in Ohio AFL-CIO Papers, Box 48, Ohio Historical Society; *Home Front* (9), October 28, 1958.

34. Letter from Charles Baker to Frank Winn, September 25, 1958, Charles Baker Papers, Box 4, Walter P. Reuther Labor Archives.

35. "Campaign Report to UOLO," Charles Baker Papers.

36. Davies, *Defender of the Old Guard*, p. 202.

37. Van Tine et al., *In the Workers' Interest*, p. 20. While 1958 turned into a Democratic year nationally, pro-labor voting on right-to-work in Ohio outpaced that in every other state with the exception of Washington State.

38. Teamster locals in the state campaigned separately and were not involved with UOLO.

39. Ted W. Brown, *Ohio Election Statistics* (Ohio Secretary of State, 1958); Van Tine et al., *In the Workers Interest*, 22; Zavacky, *Interest Groups in the Initiative Referendum Process*, 129.

40. Letter from Roy Reuther to Walter Reuther, August 8, 1958, Citizenship Department Records, UAW President's Files, Box 51, Folder 7, Walter P. Reuther Labor Archives.

41. Louis Harris and Associates, "A Study of Issues and Candidates in Ohio."

42. See Donald E. Stokes, *Voting Research and the American Businessman* (Ann Arbor, MI: Foundation for Research on Human Behavior, 1960), 22. While Ohio was a model campaign in many respects, it relied heavily on professional staff, especially at the outset. As Jane McAlevey's work shows, this kind of mobilization is unlikely to develop the ties and leaders needed to sustain a pro-labor coalition for the long haul. See *No Shortcuts: Organizing for Power in the New Gilded Age* (New York: Oxford University Press, 2016).

43. This is consistent with Fenton's analysis showing Catholics as the major source of support for labor in this contest. See John H. Fenton, "The Right-to-Work Vote in Ohio,"

Midwest Journal of Political Science 3 (1959): 241–253. I also considered county-level and campaign-specific differences from a regression of pro-labor voting across Ohio counties for the three major labor elections of the 1950s: Taft's reelection campaign in 1950, the SUBs initiative over unemployment in 1955, and right-to-work in 1958. Even after controlling for manufacturing, and for historically conservative counties where labor does worse and counties with large Catholic populations where labor typically does better, the differences across campaigns are marked. Labor's performance on right-to-work improved by up to 30 percent compared to the Taft and SUBs outcomes. This across-the-board switch in labor's performance is unlikely without the considerable labor expertise brought to bear in the 1958 campaign. County data were compiled from the Ohio Secretary of State; *Home Front*; US Department of Commerce, City and County Databook; Association of Religion Data Archives, www.TheARDA.com; Congressional Quarterly, *Voting and Elections Collection*.

44. Zavacky, *Interest Groups in the Initiative Referendum Process*, 35.
45. Congressional Quarterly, *Voting and Elections Collection*.
46. Stokes, *Voting Research and the American Businessman*, 23. CQ data on elections.
47. Van Tine et al., *In the Workers Interest*; Zimmerman, *Call Me Mike*.
48. "Burke To Seek Amendment on Right to Work," *Chicago Daily Tribune*, October 22, 1957, p. A4; "G.O.P. in Wisconsin Heals Rift by Indorsing Steinle," *Chicago Daily Tribune*, May 25, 1958, p. 7.

Chapter 5

1. Clemens, *The People's Lobby*.
2. Gordon M. Haferbecker, *Wisconsin Labor Laws* (Madison: The University of Wisconsin Press, 1958); John H. Fenton, *Midwest Politics* (New York: Holt, Rinehart and Winston, 1966).
3. Haferbecker, *Wisconsin Labor Laws*.
4. The state passed a "baby Wagner Act" in 1937 to facilitate private-sector collective bargaining, but it reversed course with the Employment Peace Act of 1943, which posed substantial restrictions on unions and picketing.
5. Richard C. Haney, *The Rise of Wisconsin's New Democrats: A Political Realignment in the Mid-Twentieth Century* 58 (1974–1975): 90–106; interview with John Lawton, conducted by Jim Cavanaugh, February 18, 1985, Wisconsin Democratic Party Oral History Project, Madison, Wisconsin.
6. See Robert W. Ozanne, *The Labor Movement in Wisconsin: A History* (Madison: The State Historical Society of Wisconsin, 1984). By 1962, the Wisconsin Educational Association was the second-largest labor organization in the state, through it was still primarily a professional association.
7. Ozanne, *The Labor Movement in Wisconsin*. Charles Schultz, president of the state CIO council, and his AFL counterpart George Haberman delayed the merger as long as they could in order to preserve their own positions. Yet with AFL union members outnumbering CIO union members by more than two to one, there was little to

debate and thus little contention. The federations merged in 1958 with Haberman president and Schultz executive vice president.

8. On Kohler and Robert Kennedy's visit, see Nelson Licthenstein, *The Most Dangerous Man in Detroit: Walter Reuther and the Fate of American Labor* (New York: Basic Books, 1995), Chapter 16.

9. Data on employer organization from Marc Dixon, "Union Threat, Countermovement Organization, and Labor Policy in the States, 1944–1960," *Social Problems* 57 (2010): 157–174.

10. While this spurred progressive movement in major cities, highlighted by the 1958 AFSCME-backed executive order by New York City mayor Robert Wagner Jr. granting municipal workers bargaining rights, several states went the other way and sought to stamp out all forms of union organization in the public sector.

11. William E. Mosher, J. Donald Kingsley, and O. Glenn Stahl, *Public Personnel Administration*, 3rd ed. (New York: Harper & Brothers, 1950), 329; on the emerging academic consensus on public-sector bargaining, see Joseph E. Slater, *Public Workers: Government Employee Unions, the Law, and the State, 1900–1962* (Ithaca, NY: ILR Press, 2004), Chapter 6.

12. "309, A Opens Enlightened Era," *Wisconsin City & County Union News*, July 1959, p. 4; Robert W. Ozanne, *The Labor Movement in Wisconsin: A History* (Madison: The State Historical Society of Wisconsin, 1984).

13. Slater, *Public Workers*; interview with former AFSCME education director in Wisconsin, Ron Kent, July 15, 2014.

14. Interview with Ron Kent.

15. Ozanne, *The Labor Movement in Wisconsin.*

16. Interview with John Lawton, conducted by Jim Cavanaugh, February 18, 1985, Wisconsin Democratic Party Oral History Project, Madison, Wisconsin.

17. Statements by The Wisconsin League of Municipalities and Lawton and the WCCME in Correspondence over 462-S, Wisconsin Governor Records (1951–1957; Kohler), Box 77, Folder 6, Wisconsin Historical Society.

18. Wisconsin Governor Records (1951–1957; Kohler). The comparison to private-sector union rights might have had more resonance during this period, given that nearly 70 percent of AFSCME workers were blue collar. Yet, as Slater notes, such forward-thinking arguments were drowned out by older fears about police strikes. See Slater, *Public Workers*, 164, 171.

19. Interview with Gaylord Nelson, Jim Cavanaugh, March 25, 1985, Wisconsin Democratic Party Oral History Project, Washington, DC; Doyle quote in Richard C. Haney, *The Rise of Wisconsin's New Democrats: A Political Realignment in the Mid-Twentieth Century* 58 (1974–1975): 90–106.

20. The AFL's Political Action Committee, Labor's League for Political Education, was tracking similar bills across the Midwest and pointed to Bradley in particular as an important supporter. See William McSorely, *Address to the Annual Convention of the Ohio State Federation of Labor*, Toledo, Ohio, August 8, 1955, in the *Proceedings to Annual Convention of the Ohio State Federation of Labor*. On the Caitlin Act, see Ozanne, *The Wisconsin Labor Movement.*

21. See Lichtenstein, *The Most Dangerous Man in Detroit*, 347; Rick Perlstein, *Before the Storm: Barry Goldwater and the Unmaking of American* Consensus (New York: Hill and Wang, 2001). Chamber of Commerce flyer on Herb Kohler speech in C. William O'Neill Papers, Box 43, Folder 1, *Ohio Historical Society.*

22. Fagin and Lawton statements reprinted in *Wisconsin City & County Union News*, October 1956, p. 1, 4.

23. Interview with John Lawton, Wisconsin Democratic Party Oral History Project; Ozanne, *The Labor Movement in Wisconsin*, 146; WSFL and State Industrial Union Council statements in *Wisconsin City & County Union News*, October 1956, p. 1.

24. Haney, "The Rise of Wisconsin's New Democrats."

25. "G.O.P. in Wisconsin Heals Rift by Endorsing Steinle," *Chicago Daily Tribune*, May 25, 1958, p. 7; "Steinle a Traditional Republican," *Chicago Daily Tribune*, September 28, 1958, p. 10.

26. Stanford Goltz, "Referendum Pledged on Right-to-Work Law," *Wisconsin State Journal*, May 25, 1958, p. 1.

27. "Thomson Says Lawton Tried 'Coercive' Action," *Wisconsin State Journal*, March 15, 1958, p. 3; Lew Roberts, "Steinle Blasts Proxmire Record on 'Labor Baron' Ties, Spending," *Wisconsin State Journal*, September 19, 1958, pp. 1–2.

28. Wisconsin Democratic Party State Platform adopted September 30, 1958, reprinted in *Wisconsin Blue Book* (Wisconsin Legislative Reference Library, Madison, 1960). 309-A developments covered in *Wisconsin City & County Union News*, February–July issues; Slater, *Public Workers.*

29. *Wisconsin City & County Union News*, July 1959, pp. 1–2.

30. Oberbeck quoted after the passage in the legislature in July. *Wisconsin City & County Union News*, July 1959, p. 1. The other union major union victory during the session was the repeal of the Caitlin Act, which prohibited political contributions by unions.

31. Chapter 509, *Acts of the Wisconsin Legislature* (1959). Retrieved from https://docs.legis.wisconsin.gov/1959; interview with John Lawton, Wisconsin Democratic Party Oral History Project; Slater, *Public Workers.*

32. The Wisconsin Education Association did not participate in the legislative campaign and was transitioning from a professional association into full-fledged union during the 1950s and 1960s, when they would have more members in the state than anyone but the UAW. See Ozanne, *The Wisconsin Labor Movement.*

33. Interview with John Lawton, Wisconsin Democratic Party Oral History Project.

34. Voting returns and legislator background from *Wisconsin Blue Book*, 1960.

35. *Wisconsin City & County Union News*, April 1959; Slater, *Public Workers.*

Chapter 6

1. McDonald singled out Timken of Canton, Ohio, in particular. "Union Foes Drive for Scab Laws," *Michigan AFL-CIO News*, August 28, 1958, p. 2.

2. Gilbert J. Gall, *The Politics of Right-to-Work: The Labor Federations as Special Interests, 1943–1979* (Westport, CT: Praeger, 1988).

3. The optics of NLRB's change of position as clearly partisan were not lost on the mainstream and conservative press. However, it was the first decision denying the UAW under Eisenhower's board that upended prior NLRB decisions on the agency shop. See Dell Bush Johannesen, "Recent Decisions Concerning the Agency Shop," *North Carolina Law Review* 40 (1962): 603–618.

4. Roscoe Born, "AFL-CIO Maps Drive for Repeal of States' 'Right-to-Work' Laws," *Wall Street Journal*, May 21, 1959, p. 1.

5. Boulware statement from "Notes for Statement on Right-to-Work," November 26, 1958, in Box 10, Folder 19, Lemuel R. Boulware Papers, Manuscript Collection 52, Rare Book & Manuscript Library, University of Pennsylvania. Biemiller quoted in Roscoe Born, "Labor Plans Drive in Congress on Right-to-Work," *Wall Street Journal*, November 6, 1958, p. 6.

6. George Bliss, "Pledge Racket Picket Fight in Legislature," *Chicago Daily Tribune*, January 27, 1959, p. 2; J. David Greenstone, *Labor in American Politics* (New York: Knopf, 1969), 132.

7. Group Research report on The National Right-to-Work Committee, 1962; Roscoe Born, "Right-to-Work Drive, Left for Dead in '58, Aims for a Comeback," *The Wall Street Journal*, April 19, 1961, p. 1; "Special Report from the National Right to Work Committee," January 1959, in Box 1587, Folder 208, John G. Ramsay Papers, Georgia State University Special Collections.

8. Gall, *The Politics of Right to Work*; personal interview with Indiana Manufacturers Association representative Ed Roberts, May 7, 2015.

9. See Sophia Z. Lee, "Whose Rights? Litigating the Right to Work, 1940–1980," in *The Right and Labor in America*, ed. Nelson Lichtenstein and Elizabeth Tandy Shermer (Philadelphia: University of Pennsylvania Press, 2012), 160–180.

10. Joseph A. McCartin, "The Radical Roots of Janus," *The American Prospect*, February 27, 2018.

11. *Wisconsin City & County Union News*, April 1959; Slater, *Public Workers*.

12. Robert G. Valletta and Richard B. Freeman, "The NBER Public Sector Collective Bargaining Law Data Set," in *When Public Sector Workers Unionize*, ed. Richard B. Freeman and Casey Ichniowski (Chicago: NBER and University of Chicago Press, 1988), Appendix B. On bargaining laws and their impact, see Richard B. Freeman, "Unionism Comes to the Public Sector," *Journal of Economic Literature* 24 (1986): 41–86; Gregory M. Saltzman, "Public Sector Bargaining Laws Really Matter: Evidence from Ohio and Illinois," in *When Public Sector Workers Unionize*, ed. Richard B. Freeman and Casey Ichniowski (Chicago: NBER and University of Chicago Press, 1988), Chapter 2.

13. McNair quote found on p. 425 in William F. Danaher and Marc Dixon, "Framing the Field: The Case of the 1969 Charleston Hospital Workers' Strike," *Mobilization* 22, no. 4 (2017): 417–433. On the civil rights crossover and Charleston in particular, see Leon Fink and Brian Greenberg, *Upheaval in the Quiet Zone*, 2nd ed. (Urbana: University of Illinois Press, 2009); Marc Dixon, William F. Danaher, and Ben Lennox Kail, "Allies, Targets, and the Effectiveness of Coalition Protest: A Comparative Analysis of Labor Unrest in the U.S. South," *Mobilization* 18, no. 3 (2013): 331–350.

14. See p. 5 in Paul T. David and Ralph Eisenberg, *Devaluation of the Urban and Suburban Vote: A Statistical Investigation of Long-Term Trends in State Legislative Representation* (Charlottesville: Bureau of Public Administration, University of Virginia, 1961). While almost all state legislatures favored rural districts prior to the Supreme Court's 1962 decision in *Baker V. Carr*, the Midwest performed relatively well. In 1955, David and Esienberg's index of representativeness put Wisconsin in the top four and Indiana, Illinois, and Michigan in the top third of most representative states. Ohio was the lone outlier, falling in the bottom quintile (41 out of 47 states with data).

15. On Ohio's late development, see Gregory M. Saltzman, "Public Sector Bargaining Laws Really Matter: Evidence from Ohio and Illinois," in *When Public Sector Workers Unionize*, ed. Richard B. Freeman and Casey Ichniowski (Chicago: NBER and University of Chicago Press, 1988); Warren Van Tine, C. J. Slanicka, Sandra Jordan, and Michael Pierce, *In the Workers' Interest: A History of the Ohio AFL-CIO, 1958–1998* (Columbus: Center for Labor Research, Ohio State University, 1998).

16. The Teamsters allegedly opposed early legislative proposals for public employee bargaining while opposition by the chamber of commerce was fairly subdued. See Dale G. Brickner, "The Status of Public Employee Bargaining," *Labor Law Journal* (August 1971): 492–498; Indiana State Teachers Association, *Advancing the Cause of Education: A History of the Indiana State Teachers Association, 1854–2004* (West Lafayette, IN: Purdue University Press, 2004).

17. Personal interview with Ron Kent, former AFSCME education director in Wisconsin, July 15, 2014.

18. Joseph A. McCartin, "'A Wagner Act for Public Employees': Labor's Deferred Dream and the Rise of Conservatism, 1970–1976," *The Journal of American History* 95, no. 1 (June 2008): 123–148.

19. Michigan has been written about extensively. See especially Greenstone, *Labor in American Politics*; Arthur William Kornhauser, Harold L. Sheppard, and Albert J. Mayer, *When Labor Votes: A Study of Auto Workers* (New York: University Books, 1956).

20. Greenstone, *Labor in American Politics*, 120.

21. John H. Fenton, *Midwest Politics* (New York: Holt, Rinehart and Winston, 1966).

22. Greenstone, *Labor in American Politics*, 136.

23. State AFL-CIO educational materials from *Michigan AFL-CIO News*, various issues, 1958–1961.

24. Robert W. Becker, Frieda L. Foote, Mathias Lubega, and Stephen V. Monsma, "Correlates of Legislative Voting: Michigan House of Representatives, 1954–1961," *Midwest Journal of Political Science* 6, no. 4 (1962): 384–396; Doris B. McLaughlin and Institute of Labor and Industrial Relations, *Michigan Labor: A Brief History from 1818 to the Present* (Ann Arbor: University of Michigan Press, 1970), 131.

25. On Williams and the Kohler extradition, see Nelson Lichtenstein, *The Most Dangerous Man in Detroit: Walter Reuther and the Fate of American Labor* (New York: Basic Books, 1995), 526.

26. Greenstone, *Labor in American Politics*, 123.

27. Walsh quoted in Gall, *The Politics of Right to Work*, 101. GOP platform and right-to-work reported in *Michigan AFL-CIO News*, "Hearing Fizzles Out," June 26, 1958, p. 1.

28. Scholle correspondence in UAW President's Office: Walter P. Reuther Records, Box 310, Folder 9, Walter P. Reuther Library, Wayne State University.

29. McLaughlin, *Michigan Labor*.

30. Austin Ranney, *Illinois Politics* (New York: New York University Press, 1960).

31. Saltzman, "Public Sector Bargaining Laws Really Matter."

32. Fay Calkins, *The CIO and the Democratic Party* (Chicago: University of Chicago Press, 1952); Greenstone, *Labor in American Politics*.

33. George Tagge, "Political Lookout," *The Chicago Daily Tribune*, June 8, 1957, p. 21.

34. *Chicago Daily Tribune*, "Burks to Seek Amendment on Right to Work," October 22, 1957, p. A4; *Chicago Daily Tribune*, "Right to Work Law Predicted by Donnelly," October 23, 1958, p. D7.

35. Proceedings of the Seventy-Sixth Annual Convention of the Illinois State Federation of Labor, October 6, 1958, Peoria, Illinois, p. 83.

36. Milton Derber, *Labor in Illinois: The Affluent Years, 1945–80* (Urbana: University of Illinois Press, 1989). AFSCME, which had the most to gain from the new law, assuaged the CFL's worst fears by recognizing the long-standing informal relationships between public employers and the building trades rather than advocating for a new bargaining unit.

37. Table 6.3 groups states into pro-labor and anti-labor/mixed outcomes. For the three focal states, the outcome is simply the campaign outcome. For Illinois and Michigan, I consider pro- and anti-labor activity more generally. While right-to-work efforts faded in Illinois due to countermovement divisions, the state labor movement was also deeply divided and failed to advance a pro-labor agenda. I thus place it in the "Anti-Labor/Mixed" category. The labor movement in Michigan headed the Democratic coalition, helped to forestall right-to-work, and the state was an early adopter of public-sector labor rights, putting it squarely in the "Pro-Labor" category.

38. Stepan-Norris and Southworth, "Rival Unionism and Membership Growth in the United States, 1900–2005." See also McCammon, *The U.S. Women's Jury Movements and Strategic Adaptation*.

Chapter 7

1. McAlevey, *No Shortcuts*.

2. A bill to repeal section 14(b) passed the House in 1965. President Johnson, however, was unwilling to spend the political capital to make it a fight in the Senate. Senate minority leader Everett Dirksen, an Illinois Republican, led a filibuster and the House bill never came to a vote. As Lichtenstein quips, highway beautification was among the many issues higher on the presidential agenda than Taft-Hartley reform (*State of The Union*, 191). Unions and the AFL-CIO still had significant legislative accomplishments during the decade. They were a big driver of Medicare even if they could not achieve labor law reform. See Quadagno, *One Nation Uninsured*.

3. Feigenbaum et al., "From the Bargaining Table to the Ballot Box"; Jacobs and Dixon, "Political Partisanship, Race, and Union Strength from 1970 to 2000"; Saltzman, "Public Sector Bargaining Laws Really Matter."

4. The divide between craft and industrial unions weakened while large unions that had once left the AFL-CIO (UAW) or had been expelled (Teamsters) came back into its fold in the 1980s, though the largest public-sector union in the NEA never would.

5. See Henry S. Farber and Bruce Western, "Accounting for the Decline of Unions in the Private Sector, 1973–1998," *Journal of Labor Research* XXII 3 (2001): 459–485; Windham, *Knocking on Labor's Door*, 181.

6. Lichtenstein, *State of the Union*; Martin and Dixon, "Changing to Win?"

7. The unsuccessful Missouri ballot initiative for right-to-work in 1978 was the only significant action on the issue in the Midwest in the 1970s and 1980s. On Reagan's impact on union organizing, see Tope and Jacobs, "The Politics of Union Decline."

8. See especially Stephen Franklin, *Three Strikes: Labor's Heartland Losses and What They Mean for Working Americans* (New York: Guilford Press, 2001). For a rare labor victory during these years, see Tom Juravich and Kate Bronfenbrenner, *Ravenswood: The Steelworkers' Victory and the Revival of American Labor* (Ithaca, NY: ILR Press, 1999).

9. Marc Dixon, "Union Organizing and Labor Outreach in the Contemporary United States, *Sociology Compass* 8 (2014): 1183–1190; Jack Fiorito and Paul Jarley, "Union Organizing and Membership Growth: Why Don't They Organize?" *Journal of Labor Research* 33 (2012): 461–486; Windham, *Knocking on Labor's Door*.

10. On average, unions and state labor federations became more sophisticated in their political operations during a period of decline. See Herbert B. Asher, Eric S. Heberlig, Randall B. Ripley, and Karen Snyder, *American Labor Unions in the Electoral Arena* (Lanham, MD: Rowman and Littlefield, 2001); William Form, *Segmented Labor, Fractured Politics: Labor Politics in American Life* (New York: Springer Series in Work and Industry, 1995); Daniel Galvin, "Resilience in the Rustbelt: Michigan Democrats and the UAW," Northwestern University, Institute for Policy Research Working Paper 13-04 (2013); Robert J. Hrebenar and Clive S. Thomas, eds., *Interest Group Politics in the Midwestern States* (Ames: Iowa State University Press, 1993).

11. Marick Masters and John T. Delaney, "Organized Labor's Political Scorecard," *Journal of Labor Research* XXVI 3 (2005): 364–392

12. AFP, at least, takes seriously differences in state institutions and personnel. They have hired through local Republican circles to help navigate these unique political contexts. See Theda Skocpol and Alexander Hertel-Fernandez, "The Koch Network and Republican Party Extremism," *Perspectives on Politics* 14 (2016): 681–699.

13. Indiana governor Mitch Daniels was on the early end of the rollback on labor rights by ending most public-sector collective bargaining by executive order upon taking office in 2006. See Joseph DiGrazia and Marc Dixon, "The Conservative Upsurge and Labor Policy in the States," *Work and Occupations* (2019): https://doi.org/10.1177/0730888419876970; Skocpol and Hertel-Fernandez, "The Koch Network and Republican Party Extremism."

14. Nelson Lichtenstein, "How Missouri Beat 'Right to Work,'" *Dissent Magazine*, August 14, 2018; Stein and Marley, *More Than They Bargained For*.

15. Joseph A. McCartin, "Bargaining for the Common Good," *Dissent Magazine*, Spring (2016); Andrew Wallender, "Number of Major Work Stoppages in U.S. Highest Since 2001," *Bloomberg News*, February 11, 2020, https://news.bloomberglaw.com/daily-labor-report/number-of-major-work-stoppages-in-u-s-highest-since-2001

Bibliography

Alder, Simeon, David Lagakos, and Lee Ohanian. "Competitive Pressure and the Decline of the Rust Belt: A Macroeconomic Analysis." National Bureau of Economic Research Working Paper 20538 (2014).

Amberg, Stephen. "The CIO Political Strategy in Historical Perspective: Creating a High Road Economy in the Postwar Era." In *Organized Labor and American Politics, 1894–1994: The Liberal-Labor Alliance*, edited by Kevin Boyle, 159–194. Albany: State University of New York Press, 1998.

Amenta, Edwin. *When Movements Matter: The Townsend Plan and the Rise of Social Security.* Princeton, NJ: Princeton University Press, 2006.

Anderson, David M. "'Things Are Different Down Here': The 1955 Perfect Circle Strike, Conservative Civic Identity, and the Roots of the New Right in the 1950s Industrial Heartland." *International Labor and Working-Class History* 74 (2008): 101–123.

Andrews, Kenneth T. "Social Movements and Policy Implementation: The Mississippi Civil Rights Movement and the War on Poverty, 1965–1971." *American Sociological Review* 66 (2001): 71–95.

Aronowitz, Stanley. *False Promises: The Shaping of American Working Class Consciousness.* New York: McGraw-Hill, 1973.

Asher, Herbert B., Eric S. Heberlig, Randall B. Ripley, and Karen Snyder. *American Labor Unions in the Electoral Arena.* Lanham, MD: Rowman and Littlefield, 2001.

Ayer, Hugh M. "Hoosier Labor in the Second World War." *Indiana Magazine of History* LIX (1963): 95–120.

Becker, Robert W., Frieda L. Foote, Mathias Lubega, and Stephen V. Monsma. "Correlates of Legislative Voting: Michigan House of Representatives, 1954–1961." *Midwest Journal of Political Science* 6 (1962): 384–396.

Bell, Daniel. *The End of Ideology.* Glencoe, IL: The Free Press, 1960.

Bernstein, Mary. "Celebration and Suppression: The Strategic Uses of Identity by the Lesbian and Gay Movement." *American Journal of Sociology* 103 (1997): 531–565.

Boryczka, Raymond, and Lorin Lee Cary. *No Strength without Union: An Illustrated History of Ohio Workers, 1803–1980.* Columbus: The Ohio Historical Society, 1982.

Boulware, Lemuel R. "Big Industry in the Community: General Electric Assesses Community Relations." *Journal of Educational Sociology* 27 (Dec. 1953): 152–159.

Bowen, Michael. "Addition through Division: Robert Taft, the Labor Vote, and the Ohio Senate Election of 1950." *Ohio Valley History* 5 (2005): 21–42.

Bowles, Samuel, David Gordon, and Thomas Weisskopf. *Beyond the Wasteland: A Democratic Alternative to Economic Decline.* New York: Anchor Press, 1983.

Brady, David, Regina S. Baker, and Ryan Finnigan. "When Unionization Disappears: State-Level Unionization and Working Poverty in the United States." *American Sociological Review* 78 (2013): 872–896.

Brickner, Dale G. "The Status of Public Employee Bargaining." *Labor Law Journal* (August 1971): 492–498.

Burstein, Paul. *American Public Opinion, Advocacy, and Policy in Congress: What the Public Wants and What It Gets*. New York: Cambridge University Press, 2014.

Bush Johannesen, Dell. "Recent Decisions Concerning the Agency Shop." *North Carolina Law Review* 40 (1962): 605–618.

Calkins, Fay. *The CIO and the Democratic Party*. Chicago: University of Chicago Press, 1952.

Campbell, John. *American Discontent: The Rise of Donald Trump and the Decline of the Golden Age*. New York: Oxford University Press, 2018.

Cayton, Andrew. *Ohio: The History of a People*. Columbus: The Ohio State University Press, 2002.

Clawson, Dan. *The Next Upsurge: Labor and the New Social Movements*. Ithaca, NY: ILR Press, 2003.

Clawson, Dan, and Mary Ann Clawson. "What Has Happened to the US Labor Movement? Union Decline and Renewal." *Annual Review of Sociology* 25 (1999): 95–119.

Clemens, Elisabeth. *The People's Lobby: Organizational Innovation and the Rise of Interest Group Politics in the United States, 1890-1925*. Chicago: The University of Chicago Press, 1997.

Cowie, Jefferson. *The Great Exception*. Princeton, NJ: Princeton University Press, 2016.

Cress, Daniel M., and David A. Snow. "The Outcomes of Homeless Mobilization: The Influence of Organization, Disruption, Political Mediation, and Framing." *American Journal of Sociology* 105 (2000): 1063–1104.

Danaher, William F., and Marc Dixon. "Framing the Field: The Case of the 1969 Charleston Hospital Worker's Strike." *Mobilization* 22 (2017): 417–433.

Dark, Taylor. *The Unions and the Democrats: An Enduring Alliance*. Ithaca, NY: ILR Press, 1999.

Dauer, Manning. "Recent Southern Political Thought." *Journal of Politics* 10 (1948): 327–353.

David, Paul T., and Ralph Eisenberg. *Devaluation of the Urban and Suburban Vote: A Statistical Investigation of Long-Term Trends in State Legislative Representation*. Charlottesville: Bureau of Public Administration, University of Virginia, 1961.

Davies, Richard O. *Defender of the Old Guard: John Bricker and American Politics*. Columbus: Ohio State University Press, 1993.

Davis, Mike. *Prisoners of the American Dream*. London: Verso, 1986.

de Leon, Cedric. *The Origins of Right-to-Work: Anti-Labor Democracy in Nineteenth Century Chicago*. Ithaca, NY: ILR Press, 2015.

Derber, Milton. *Labor in Illinois: the Affluent Years, 1945-1980*. Urbana: University of Illinois Press, 1989.

DiGrazia, Joseph, and Marc Dixon. "The Conservative Upsurge and Labor Policy in the States." *Work and Occupations* (2019): https://doi.org/10.1177/0730888419876970.

Dixon, Marc. "Limiting Labor: Business Political Mobilization and Union Setback in the States." *Journal of Policy History* 19 (2007): 313–344.

Dixon, Marc. "Movements, Countermovements, and Policy Adoption: The Case of Right-to-Work Activism." *Social Forces* 87 (2008): 473–500.

Dixon, Marc. "Union Organizing and Labor Outreach in the Contemporary United States." *Sociology Compass* 8 (2014): 1183–1190.

Dixon, Marc. "Union Threat, Countermovement Organization, and Labor Policy in the States, 1944-1960." *Social Problems* 57 (2010): 157–174.

Dixon, Marc, William F. Danaher, and Ben Lennox Kail. "Allies, Targets, and the Effectiveness of Coalition Protest: A Comparative Analysis of Labor Unrest in the US South." *Mobilization* 18 (2013): 331–350.

Dixon, Marc, and Andrew W. Martin. "'We Can't Win This on Our Own': Unions, Firms, and the Mobilization of External Allies in Labor Disputes." *American Sociological Review* 77 (2012): 946–969.

Dubofsky, Melvin, and Warren Van Tine. *John L. Lewis: A Biography.* Urbana: University of Illinois Press, 1986.

Eidlin, Barry. *Labor and the Class Idea in the United States and Canada.* Cambridge: Cambridge University Press, 2018.

Evans, Thomas W. *The Education of Ronald Reagan: The General Electric Years and the Untold Story of his Conversion to Conservatism.* New York: Columbia University Press, 2006.

Farber, Henry S., and Bruce Western. "Accounting for the Decline of Unions in the Private Sector, 1973–1998." *Journal of Labor Research* XXII 3 (2001): 459–485.

Feigenbaum, James, Alexander Hertel-Fernandez, and Vanessa Williamson. "From the Bargaining Table to the Ballot Box: Political Effects of Right to Work Laws." National Bureau of Economic Research Working Paper 24259 (2018).

Fenton, John H. *Midwest Politics.* New York: Holt, Rinehart and Winston, 1966.

Fink, Leon, and Brian Greenberg. *Upheaval in the Quiet Zone.* 2nd ed. Urbana: University of Illinois Press, 2009.

Fiorito, Jack. "The State of the Unions." *Journal of Labor Research* 28 (2007): 43–68.

Fiorito, Jack, and Paul Jarley. "Union Organizing and Membership Growth: Why Don't They Organize?" *Journal of Labor Research* 33 (2012): 461–486.

Fones-Wolf, Elizabeth A. *Selling Free Enterprise.* Urbana: University of Illinois Press, 1994.

Form, William. *Segmented Labor, Fractured Politics: Labor Politics in American Life.* New York: Springer, 1995.

Franklin, Stephen. *Three Strikes: Labor's Heartland Losses and What They Mean for Working Americans.* New York: The Guilford Press, 2001.

Freeman, Richard B. "Unionism Comes to the Public Sector." *Journal of Economic Literature* 24 (1986): 41–86.

Freeman, Richard B., Eunice Han, David Madland, and Brendan V. Duke. "How Does Declining Unionism Affect the American Middle Class and Intergenerational Mobility?" National Bureau of Economic Research Working Paper 21638 (Oct. 2015).

Freeman, Richard B., and Casey Ichniowski, eds. *When Public Employees Unionize* Chicago: NBER and University of Chicago Press, 1988.

Freeman, Richard B., and James L. Medoff. *What Do Unions Do?* New York: Basic Books, 1984.

Galbraith, John Kenneth. *American Capitalism: The Concept of Countervailing Power.* Boston: Houghton Mifflin, 1952.

Gall, Gilbert J. *The Politics of Right-to-Work: The Labor Federations and Special Interests, 1943–1979.* New York: Greenwood Press, 1988.

Gall, Gilbert J. "Thoughts on Defeating Right-to-Work: Reflections on Two Referendum Campaigns." In *Organized Labor and American Politics, 1894–1994: The Labor-Liberal Alliance,* edited by Kevin Boyle, 195–216. Albany, NY: State University of New York Press, 1998.

Galvin, Daniel. "Resilience in the Rustbelt: Michigan Democrats and the UAW." Northwestern University, Institute for Policy Research Working Paper 13-04 (2013).

Ganz, Marshal. *Why David Sometimes Wins*. New York: Oxford University Press, 2009.

Godard, John. "The Exceptional Decline of the American Labor Movement." *Industrial and Labor Relations Review* 63 (2009): 82–108.

Goldfield, Michael. *The Decline of Organized Labor in the United States*. Chicago: University of Chicago Press, 1987.

Greenstone, J. David. *Labor and American Politics*. New York: Random House, 1979.

Haferbecker, Gordon M. *Wisconsin Labor Laws*. Madison: The University of Wisconsin Press, 1958.

Haney, Richard C. "The Rise of Wisconsin's New Democrats: A Political Realignment in the Mid-Twentieth Century." *Wisconsin Magazine of History* 58 (1974–75): 90-106.

Hissam, Michael B. *C. William O'Neill and the 1958 Right-to-Work Amendment*. Honors Thesis, Department of History, The Ohio State University, 2005.

Howell, John Harris. *The Right to Manage: Industrial Relations Policies of American Business in the 1940s*. Madison: University of Wisconsin Press, 1982.

Hrebenar, Robert J., and Clive S. Thomas, eds. *Interest Group Politics in the Midwestern States*. Ames: Iowa State University Press, 1993.

Indiana State Teachers Association. *Advancing the Cause of Education: A History of the Indiana State Teachers Association, 1854–2004*. West Lafayette, IN: Purdue University Press, 2004.

Isaac, Larry, and Lars Christiansen. "How the Civil Rights Movement Revitalized Labor Militancy." *American Sociological Review* 67 (2002): 722–746.

Isaac, Larry, Steve McDonald, and Greg Lukasik. "Takin' It from the Streets: How the Sixties Mass Movement Revitalized Unionization." *American Journal of Sociology* 112 (2006): 46–96.

Jacobs, David, and Marc Dixon. "Political Partisanship and Union Strength from 1970 to 2002: A Pooled Time-Series Analysis." *Social Science Research* 39 (2010): 1059–1072.

Jacobs, David, and Marc Dixon. "The Politics of Labor-Management Relations: Detecting the Conditions that Affect Changes in Right-to-Work Laws." *Social Problems* 53 (2006): 118–137.

Juravich, Tom, and Kate Bronfenbrenner. *Ravenswood: The Steelworkers' Victory and the Revival of American Labor*. Ithaca, NY: ILR Press, 1999.

Kahn, Melvin. *The Politics of American Labor: The Indiana Microcosm*. Carbondale: Southern Illinois University Labor Institute, 1970.

Kerr, Clark, ed. *Labor and Management in Industrial Society*. New York: Anchor, 1964.

Kimeldorf, Howard. "Worker Replacement Costs and Unionization: Origins of the U.S. Labor Movement." *American Sociological Review* 78 (2013): 1033–1062.

King, Brayden G., and Nicholas Pearce. "The Contentiousness of Markets: Politics, Social Movements, and Institutional Change in Markets." *Annual Review of Sociology* 36 (2010): 249–267.

Korstad, Robert, and Nelson Lichtenstein. "Opportunities Found and Lost: Labor, Radicals, and the Early Civil Rights Movement." *The Journal of American History* 75 (1988): 786–811.

Kotz, David M. *The Rise and Fall of Neoliberal Capitalism*. Cambridge, MA: Harvard University Press, 2015.

Lafer, Gordon. "The Legislative Attack on American Wages and Labor Standards, 2011–2012." *Economic Policy Institute* (2013), Briefing Paper #364.

Lee, Sophia Z. "Whose Rights? Litigating the Right to Work, 1940–1980." In *The Right and Labor in America*, edited by Nelson Lichtenstein and Tandy Shermer, 160–180. Philadelphia: University of Pennsylvania Press, 2012.

Lichtenstein, Nelson. *The Most Dangerous Man in Detroit: Walter Reuther and the Fate of American Labor*. New York: Basic Books, 1995.

Lichtenstein, Nelson. *State of the Union*. Princeton, NJ: Princeton University Press, 2002.

Lichtenstein, Nelson, and Elizabeth Tandy Shermer, eds. *The Right and Labor in America*. Philadelphia: University of Pennsylvania Press, 2012.

Lipold, Paul, and Larry Isaac. "Striking Deaths: Lethal Contestation and the 'Exceptional' Character of the American Labor Movement, 1870–1970." *International Review of Social History* 54 (2009): 167–205.

Lubell, Samuel. *The Future of American Politics*. New York: Harper, 1951.

Lynd, Robert S., and Helen Lynd. *Middletown: A Study in Contemporary American Culture*. New York: Harcourt, Brace, and Company, 1929.

Martin, Andrew W., and Marc Dixon. "Changing to Win? Resistance, Threat and the Role of Unions in Strikes, 1984–2002." *American Journal of Sociology* 116: 93–129.

Martin, John Bartlow. *Indiana: An Interpretation*. New York: Alfred A. Knopf, 1947.

Masters, Marick, and John T. Delaney. "Organized Labor's Political Scorecard." *Journal of Labor Research* XXVI 3 (2005): 364–392.

Mayhew, David R. *Placing Parties in American Politics: Organization, Electoral Settings, and Government Activity in the Twentieth Century*. Princeton, NJ: Princeton University Press, 1986.

McAdam, Doug. *Political Process and the Development of Black Insurgency, 1930–1970*. Chicago: University of Chicago Press, 1999.

McAdam, Doug, and Hilary Schaffer Boudet. *Putting Movements in Their Place: Explaining Opposition to Energy Projects in the United States, 2000–2005*. New York: Cambridge University Press, 2012.

McAlevey, Jane F. *No Shortcuts: Organizing for Power in the New Gilded Age*. New York: Oxford University Press, 2016.

McCammon, Holly J. "Disorganizing and Reorganizing Conflict: Outcomes of the State's Legal Regulation of the Strike Since the Wagner Act." *Social Forces* 72 (1994): 1011–1049.

McCammon, Holly J. *The U.S. Women's Jury Movements and Strategic Adaptation: A More Just Verdict*. New York: Cambridge University Press, 2012.

McCarthy, John D., and Mayer N. Zald. "Resource Mobilization and Social Movements: A Partial Theory." *American Journal of Sociology* 82 (1977): 1212–1241.

McCartin, Joseph A. "'A Wagner Act for Public Employees': Labor's Deferred Dream and the Rise of Conservatism, 1970–1976." *The Journal of American History* (June 2008): 123–148.

McCartin, Joseph A., and Jean-Christian Vinel. "'Compulsory Unionism': Sylvester Petro and the Career of an Anti-Union Idea, 1957–1987." In *The Right and Labor in America*, edited by Nelson Lichtenstein and Elizabeth Tandy Shermer, 226–251. Philadelphia: University of Pennsylvania Press, 2012.

McGlaughlin, Doris B. *Michigan Labor: A Brief History from 1880 to the Present*. Ann Arbor: Institute for Labor and Industrial Relations, University of Michigan-Wayne State University, 1970.

McQuarrie, Michael. "The Revolt of the Rust Belt: Place and Politics in the Age of Anger." *The British Journal of Sociology* 68 (2017): S120–S152.

McVeigh, Rory. *The Rise of the Ku Klux Klan: Right-Wing Movements in National Politics.* Minneapolis: University of Minnesota Press, 2009.

Meyer, David S. *The Politics of Protest: Social Movements in America.* New York: Oxford University Press, 2007.

Meyer, David S. "Protest and Political Opportunities." *Annual Review of Sociology* 30 (2007): 125–145.

Meyer, David, and Suzanne Staggenborg. "Movements, Countermovements, and the Structure of Political Opportunity." *American Journal of Sociology* 101 (1996): 1628–1660.

Meyer, David S., and Sidney Tarrow. "A Movement Society: Contentious Politics for a New Century." In *The Social Movement Society*, edited by David S. Meyer and Sidney Tarrow, 1–28. Lanham, MD: Rowman and Littlefield, 1998.

Miller, Glen W., and Stephen B. Ware. "Organized Labor in the Political Process: A Case Study of the Right-to-Work Campaign in Ohio." *Labor History* 4 (1963): 51–67.

Mills, C. Wright. "Letter to the New Left." *New Left Review* I (1960): 18–23.

Mills, C. Wright. *The New Men of Power.* Urbana: University of Illinois Press, (1948) 2001.

Nissen, Bruce. A Post-World War II 'Social Accord?'" In *U.S. Labor Relations, 1945–1989: Accommodation and Conflict*, edited by Bruce Nissen, 173–205. New York: Garland, 1990.

Offe, Claus, and Helmut Wiesenthal. "Two Logics of Collective Action: Theoretical Notes on Social Class and Organizational Form." *Political Power and Social Theory* 1 (1980): 67–115.

Ozanne, Robert W. *The Labor Movement in Wisconsin: A History.* Madison: The State Historical Society of Wisconsin, 1984.

Pacewiz, Josh. *Partisans and Partners: The Politics of the Post-Keynesian Society* Chicago: The University of Chicago Press, 2016.

Perlstein, Rick. *Before the Storm: Barry Goldwater and the Unmaking of the American Consensus.* New York: Farrar, Straus and Giroux, 2001.

Petro, Sylvester. *The Kohler Strike: Union Violence and Administrative Law.* Chicago: H. Regnery Co., 1961.

Petro, Sylvester. *The Labor Policy of the Free Society.* New York: Ronald Press, 1957.

Phillips-Fein, Kim. *Invisible Hands: The Businessmen's Crusade against the New Deal.* New York: W.W. Norton & Company, 2010.

Polsby, Nelson W. "How to Study Community Power: The Pluralist Alternative." *Journal of Politics* 22 (1960): 474–484.

Putnam, Robert. *Our Kids: The American Dream in Crisis.* New York: Simon & Schuster, 2016.

Quadagno, Jill. *One Nation Uninsured.* New York: Oxford University Press, 2004.

Ranney, Austin. *Illinois Politics.* New York: New York University Press, 1960.

Reuschemeyer, Dietrich. "Can One or a Few Cases Yield Theoretical Gains." In *Comparative Historical Analysis in the Social Sciences*, edited by James Mahoney and Dietrich Rueschemeyer, 305–336. New York: Cambridge University Press, 2003.

Rogers, Joel. "Divide and Conquer: Further 'Reflections on the Distinctive Character of American Labor Laws.'" *University of Wisconsin Law Review* (1990): 1–147.

Rosenfeld, Jake. *What Unions No Longer Do.* Cambridge, MA: Harvard University Press, 2014.

Rubin, Beth. "Class Struggle American Style: Unions, Strikes, and Wages." *American Sociological Review* 51 (1986): 618–633.

Saltzman, Gregory M. "Public Sector Bargaining Laws Really Matter: Evidence from Ohio and Illinois." In *When Public Sector Workers Unionize*, edited by Richard B. Freeman and Casey Ichniowski, 41–80. Chicago: University of Chicago Press, 1988.

Schattschneider, E. E. *The Semisovereign People*. New York: Holt, Rinehart and Winston, 1960.

Schlozman, Daniel. *When Movements Anchor Parties: Electoral Alignments in American History*. Princeton, NJ: Princeton University Press, 2015.

Scipes, Kim. "It's Time to Come Clean: Open the AFL-CIO Archives on International Labor Operations." *Labor Studies Journal* 25, no. 2 (2000): 4–25.

Skocpol, Theda, and Alexander Hertel-Fernandez. "The Koch Network and Republican Party Extremism." *Perspectives on Politics* 14 (2016): 681–699.

Slater, Joseph E. *Public Workers: Government Employee Unions, the Law, and the State, 1900–1962*. Ithaca, NY: ILR Press, 2004.

Snow, David A., E. Burke Rochford, Jr., Steven K. Worden, and Robert D. Benford. "Frame Alignment Processes, Micromobilization and Movement Participation." *American Sociological Review* 51 (1986): 546–548.

Soule, Sara A., and Brayden G. King. "The Stages of the Policy Process and the Equal Rights Amendment, 1972–1982." *American Journal of Sociology* 111 (2006): 1871–1909.

Stein, Jason, and Patrick Marley. *More Than They Bargained For: Scott Walker, Unions, and the Fight for Wisconsin*. Madison: University of Wisconsin Press, 2013.

Stepan-Norris, Judith, and Caleb Southworth. "Rival Unionism and Membership Growth in the United States, 1900–2005." *American Sociological Review* 75 (2010): 227–251.

Stepan-Norris, Judith, and Maurice Zeitlin. *Left Out: Reds and America's Industrial Unions*. New York: Cambridge University Press, 2003.

Stokes, Donald E. *Voting Research and the American Businessman*. Ann Arbor, MI: Foundation for Research on Human Behavior, 1960.

Sweeney, John J., and Karen Nussbaum. *Solution for the New Workforce*. Cabin John, MD: Seven Locks Press, 1989.

Thelen, Kathleen. *Varieties of Liberalization and the New Politics of Social Solidarity*. Cambridge: Cambridge University Press, 2014.

Tilly, Charles, and Lesley J. Wood. *Social Movements, 1768–2008*. Boulder, CO: Paradigm, 2009.

Troy, Leo. *Trade Union Membership, 1897–1962*. New York: National Bureau of Economic Research, 1965.

Van Tine, Warren, C. J. Slanicka, Sandra Jordan, and Michale Pierce. *In the Workers' Interest: A History of the Ohio AFL-CIO, 1958–1998*. Columbus: Center for Labor Research, Ohio State University, 1998.

Varga, Joseph. "Dispossession Is Nine-tenths of the Law: Right-to-Work and the Making of the American Precariat." *Labor Studies Journal* 39 (2014): 25–45.

Walker, Edward T. *Grassroots for Hire: Public Affairs Consultants in American Democracy*. New York: Cambridge University Press, 2014.

Western, Bruce. *Between Class and Market: Postwar Unionization in the Capitalist Democracies*. Princeton, NJ: Princeton University Press, 1997.

Western, Bruce, and Jake Rosenfeld. "Unions, Norms, and the Rise in U.S. Wage Inequality." *American Sociological Review* 76 (2011): 513–537.

Windham, Lane. *Knocking on Labor's Door: Union Organizing in the 1970s and the Roots of a New Economic Divide*. Chapel Hill: University of North Carolina Press, 2017.

Wuerthner, J. J. *The Businessman's Guide to Practical Politics*. Chicago: H. Regnery Co., 1959.

Zald, Mayer N., and Burt Useem. "Movement and Countermovement Interaction: Mobilization, Tactics, and State Involvement." In *Social Movements in an Organizational Society*, edited by Mayer N Zald and John McCarthy, 247–272. New Brunswick, NJ: Transaction Books, 1987.

Zavacky, Michael James. *Interest Groups in the Initiative Referendum Process*. PhD Dissertation, University of Pittsburgh, 1968.

Index

Tables and figures are indicated by *t* and *f* following the page number

For the benefit of digital users, indexed terms that span two pages (e.g., 52–53) may, on occasion, appear on only one of those pages.